Designerly Entrepreneurship

Accelerate actions, get real skin in the game and let customers evaluate with their wallets to drive fast, focused and valid product development.

Designerly Entrepreneurship
By Christian Tollestrup and Linda Nhu Laursen

1st Edition, 1st Print Run

© The Authors and Aalborg University Press, 2022

Graphic design: Quang Tran
Printed by Toptryk Grafisk Aps, 2022
ISBN: 978-87-7210-759-2

Photos which are not marked with a particular photographer are the individual students' own photos, which the chapter is based upon.

Published by Aalborg University Press | forlag.aau.dk

The book is financially supported by Department of Architecture, Design & Media Technology, Aalborg University

All rights reserved. No part of this book may be reprinted or reproduced or utilized in any form or by any electronic, mechanical, or other means, now known or hereafter invented, including photocopying and recording, or in any information storage or retrieval system, without permission in writing from the publishers, except for reviews and short excerpts in scholarly publications.

Designerly Entrepreneurship

Define, design and make 20 pieces of a product in 10 days and sell it at designers market.

Christian Tollestrup & Linda Nhu Laursen

AALBORG UNIVERSITY PRESS

- Mark will be joining your journey in the Designerly Entrepreneurship Challenge

Contents

11	**Section I · The Challenge**
12	Why an entrepreneurship challenge for designers?
18	The Designerly Entrepreneurship Challenge
34	Why a designerly challenge?
43	**Section II · The Cases**
44	Cases Analysis Structure
46	Case aspects – The pressure cooker
50	Case: The Hanging/Table Lamp
60	Case: Wall Cushions
70	Case: Hydroponic Pots
82	Case: Wall Clock
90	Case: Table lamp 1
102	Case: Table lamp 2
119	**Section III · The Execution**
120	Advice for staging and participating
124	Resource Worksheet
128	Production Worksheet
136	Marketing Worksheet
139	Sales Worksheet

Photo: Jonas Lundgaard Svendsen

The Challenge

Why an entrepreneurship challenge for designers?

Through the years, we have educated more than 400 designers. When designers progress through their education, they - as most other profession - progress from novice to becoming a competent professional or even an expert by acquiring the skills and competences of their profession (Dreyfus and Dreyfus, 1980). Design courses and literature typically teach process and methods for understanding three core aspects (Brown and Katz, 2011):

- The desirability, often based on user research
- The feasibility, principles, considerations and details on materials, construction, production and assembly, etc.
- The viability, the market and the competitive situation.

During a hands-on reflective approach designers gradually learn to see, understand and interact with the world through a designerly paradigm (Laursen and Tollestrup, 2017).

Designer bias

We have however discovered a pitfall in this development of design expertise: when there is a large risk, designers develop a bias. While we talk about design as a holistic, iterative, materialising discipline, many design models, processes, and projects tend to focus and emphasize on the product use – that is the user and desirability aspects - neglecting the business aspects that is crucial for realising innovations (Buijs, 2012). When starting with the user's perspective rather than the perspective of the customer, the production aspects come later in the development process, and then maybe the business aspects are addressed at the very end. Ultimately, this results in many design projects not prioritising the business aspects.

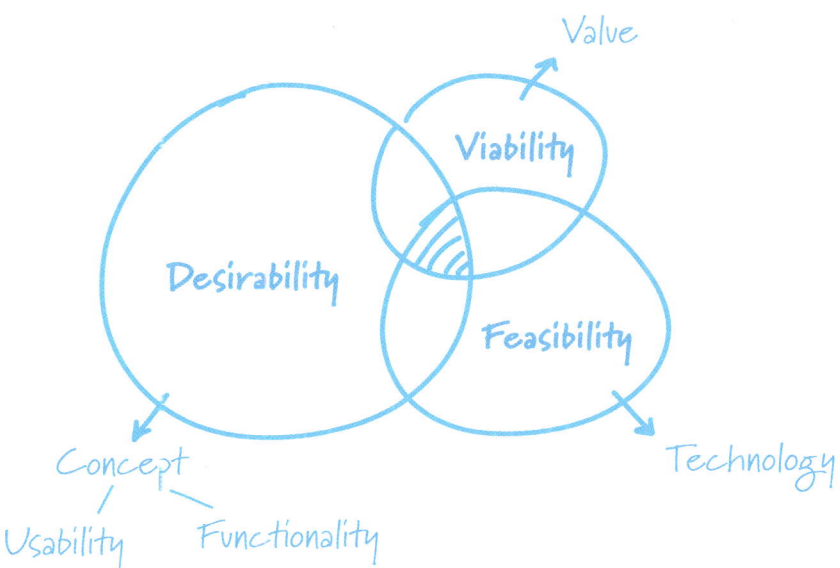

With minor focus on the business aspect, many designers end up doing desirable representations. They create design-proposals that are nicely rendered, 3D printed and presented in a persuasive pitch, but may be far from the current business reality. While production for design engineering may be somewhat integrated (Ulrich and Eppinger, 2003), in particular the business dimensions are handled at arm's length, without taking full responsibility for important details that are critical and very costly for realising the product. In other words, while being desirable, many designed products are at risk of being detached from the business reality.
So, we asked:

> How can we ensure that designers end up dealing with real problems, real matters, real questions?
> How can we challenge designers to design products for a business reality?

Off-set in the business

This book strives to drive designers away from a primary desirability focus, which is expressed as thought representations (drawings, renderings, presentations), toward doing realisable design. We argue that, to produce a realisable product, it is crucial to consider everything simultaneously and in a real business context. When developing a product design, you need to consider the business, the risk, the investment, the purchasing, the sales situation, the production, the value chain, etc., no field can be overlooked. So, our quest becomes to frame a real challenge that aligns the designers with managers, business owners, innovators, developers, engineers, etc.

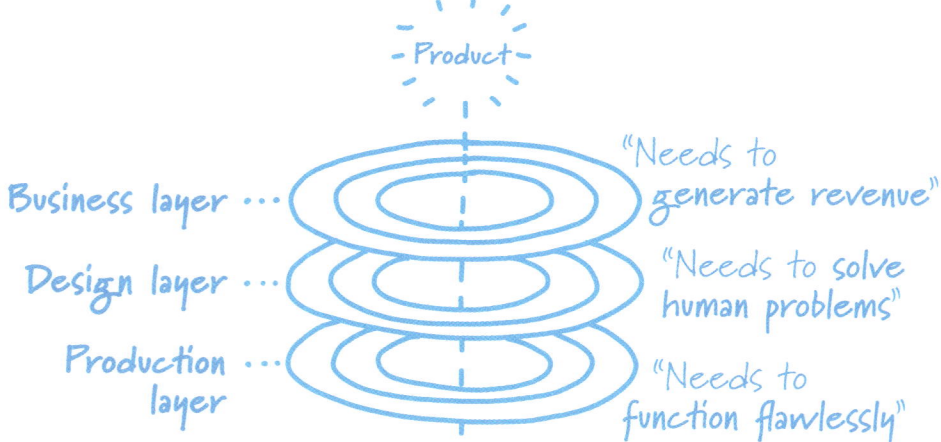

Designers know that a company (clients) will have to execute on the idea for a product. They will have to deal with the uncertainties of interrelated issues, such as market size, customers' willingness to buy, the challenges of setting up production and production lines, marketing strategies, logistics, etc. They know this intellectually. But do they know it for real? Have they felt it? It is not enough to only consider everything on paper, in desktop-analytical mode, you need to do it for real. We discovered, that in many cases the problems and objections from business owners, purchasers and investors are not always taken seriously. Many design students have not felt the risk and faced the uncertainty or the responsibility when there is something real at stake. Real business ownership. It is not something they have dealt with personally—until now.

We promise real ownership

In this book, we pose a challenge that shifts the objective from focusing on a fragmented design task to completing the end-to-end target of designing and selling a product. The challenge will require you to adopt all the roles entailed in product design, production and selling. Our experience is that when designers take sole ownership of all the problems in bringing the products to market, they cannot push them on to others, and this drives real integration of design, business and production. It will tie together the real-life aspect of defining, investing, designing, purchasing, production, promoting and selling a product in a concrete and tangible but still manageable way.

We pose a framed challenge that will force you to define, design, make and sell 20 pieces of a real product in 10 days. The aim is to push designers to have skin in the game, feel ownership for the business and production issues; to become the investor and business owner; to become the producer; to become the marketing and salesperson. We want designers to understand, for real, what their focus is and why. What makes their life difficult? This challenge pushes designer to own 100% of the business. Get real skin in the game and face real customers at the end. You put real skin in the game to get real products out.

It is a time-pressured challenge to help designers focus on what matters - in reality, which is to drive real products with the business and production that this entails. Then we will avoid feature creep, unreal products and irrelevant detours, and obtain sharp simple products with maximum valuable effect. When you design for a real customer, no situation is artificial. We want designers to deal with what really matters when designing and taking a product to market.

Who is this book for?

This book is written for you, if you want to try doing business a designerly way. We wrote this book simply because we found that there is a gap in many current design theories, design processes and design models. They fail to combine the design and business aspects. The challenge presented here requires the equal balance and integration of the designerly and business aspects. This book pushes designers to design for the real world, with a 100% ownership and full consideration of the design, the business and the production aspects from the start and throughout the entire process.

Designers
We think that younger designers can make use of this book. By focusing on a holistic challenge with a hard target of delivery, the process will unfold with the use of only the most essential tools and methods. Instead of striving for that perfect process, we hope you recognise that, even though we have a design degree, we do not necessarily know the right direction from the start. There is no perfect answer. The best approach is to forge an uncharted path, taking the first step, then the next steps.

Design interested
We also wrote this book for anyone working within product development and innovation that has an interest in the design field. You may have read or heard a lot about design thinking and how that may be relevant for business and problem solving in many other fields. This book is about design-doing in a business context. The challenge is to merge a design approach with entrepreneurship and to integrate production and market aspects in the process from idea to finished product. It is not a planning and thinking approach. Instead, it is designerly; you need to get moving, get info and reconfigure your design.

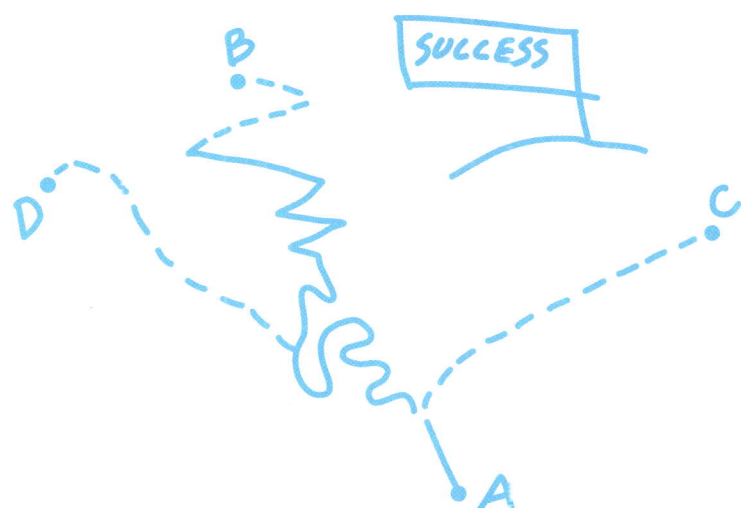

The Designerly Entrepreneurship Challenge

The Designerly Entrepreneurship challenge is a result of decades of teaching, training and conducting workshops for design students, designers, entrepreneurs, innovation managers and engineers in both an academic and industry setting.

The idea with the challenge is to emphasise the execution and action aspects of the design process. Thus, the challenge is framed to be simple enough to empower designers. It provides the freedom to choose complexity, scale, etc., depending on your ambition, resources, skills, risk willingness and network. The simplicity also enables you to focus on execution rather than dealing with extensive research, complex technology and production processes. The challenge is simple but time-pressured. It is framed to accelerate product development and drive business focus by letting the customers evaluate with a buy/no-buy decision on the real product in just 10 days.

Define, design and make 20 units of a product in 10 days, and sell it at Designers' Market.

As opposed to most students' design projects in an educational setting, where the main output is a proposal for a product, this output is a real product for real customers built with real accessible technology. Because you are 100% responsible for your own design, product, financing, marketing and production, you face all the challenges a business also faces. But, in this setting, you experience it up-close and personal and take it seriously on a whole different level. You are intrinsically motivated to create a product that customers want to buy. This facilitates your ability to focus on which solution creates the most value within the limited timeframe. That kind of objective helps you to focus your resources and activities on the most important aspects.

Simple boundaries and ground rules
Instead of detailing and outlining the specific content of the task, the framing is reversed and focuses on some simple boundaries and requirements for setting the ground rules.

Each designer (or development team) will design, produce and promote a minimum of 20 units of a product; and sell these at a Designers' Market within 10 days. Near the end of the 10 days, a timeboxed market event will be arranged where the development efforts are presented with the intention to sell. The following ground rules are established to keep things in line with the product development agenda:

Rule 1   No food.

Rule 2   If a service component is included,
         it must be consumed at the market.

Rule 3   Self-produced components must be
         a minimum of 50% of the product.

Rule 4   Don't kill people.

Rule 2 and Rule 3 prevent short-cuts, such as selling vouchers for services like designing graphics or even completely unrelated activities like cleaning. The 50% self-production rule prevents products that are just bought and traded.
Rule 1 and Rule 4 are safety measures. Selling food requires a license so that people don't get sick from wrongly treated produce. Rule 4 is common sense, but it reminds designers to be very careful with electrical components. They should not make these themselves; they should source them from other products, which also complies with Rule 2.

In the following sections, we will disseminate and explain the rationale behind each element of the challenge.

Define, design and make 20 units of a product in 10 days, and sell it at Designers' Market.

Why define, design and make?

In this design-based entrepreneurship challenge, you need to define, design and make at least 50% of the product yourself. That means you can't purchase and resell, or just repaint/modify an existing product. You need to figure out how to add enough value through design to create a value proposition that will attract real customers.

With the objective of producing actual products, you are forced to balance what you would like to make with what you can actually produce. That means there is a hard link between the design of a product and the production of the proposed design. When you must execute both aspects, you automatically consider the production aspects during the ideation phase. This brings a whole new range of parameters such as resources, competences, capabilities etc. to the forefront of the design process, where designers tend to mostly focus on user needs and desires.

Understanding the realities of production

The scope of what product to make is heavily influenced by what you can do yourself or whom you know that can help with the materials, production and promotion activities. Production processes, materials and tools are no longer an academic reflection, but a hardcore parameter directly influencing the choice of product type and other design decisions. You will experience that ideas are no longer evaluated for their user-value alone; they are also evaluated against what production processes you master and what materials you can source. These aspects make designers and developers balance their product design with their capabilities and resources, their abilities to execute the proposal, and, to some extent, almost reverse engineer their proposal from what they can do.

Define, design and make **20 units** of a product in 10 days, and sell it at Designers' Market.

Why 20 units?

Industrial design is about designing for scaled production, i.e. taking production processes into account when designing the product. The challenge of making 20 units is enough to mimic industrial production at an individual scale, given the timeframe. It considers the concept versus the actual product and the compromises you must make.
There is enough repetition to introduce the concept of production planning, allocation of time and resources to complete the production processes on time. With 20 units, rather than five, it is hard to avoid the task of planning the activities; consequently, it makes sense to plan so time is not wasted.

Considering risk and consistency

The higher number of units also introduces more risk that something can go wrong in the process and affect the outcome. We find that this compels you to pay more attention to the production; both the planning and execution becomes a higher priority from the very beginning. Making 20 identical pieces also introduces the element of consistency and risk. Making 20 pieces by hand in the workshop, even when using CNC-milling, laser-cutting and 3D printing, still requires time for polishing/post-processing to achieve the same quality in all of the units. The output of these machines might require more post-processing by hand in order to achieve acceptable surface quality. Also extensive or advanced functionality may be hard to achieve. These considerations force you to more critically consider the desired aesthetics and functionality and ask: "Is this absolutely necessary?"

Define, design and make 20 units **of a product** in 10 days, and sell it at Designers' Market.

Why any product?

Instead of detailing and outlining the specific content of the task, the framing is reversed and focuses on the ground rules, setting some simple boundaries and requirements. This has multiple benefits that add up to freedom of choice.

Ownership and ambition
The first benefit is freedom. You are free to calibrate and choose the complexity and scale of your own challenge. It will depend on your own level of ambition, confidence, skills, network possibilities and risk willingness—financially and timewise. When you are given this freedom, you also have full ownership of all decisions (and the rewards). There are no arbitrary boundaries, and ambitious and risk willing people can work side by side with less ambitious and less risk willing people but have the same experience of designing and producing a product.

Pragmatism
The second reason is that this approach is pragmatic. With different and limited capacity, a well-defined product as a set task could risk creating bottlenecks in the production if everyone chose to go through the same production processes. Instead, it supports an entrepreneurial approach by allowing you to freely utilise your unique network and resources. You are not bound by an arbitrary assignment; instead, you need to create your own opportunity.

Define, design and make 20 units of a product in 10 days, and sell it at Designers' Market.

Why 10 days?

It sounds like it is almost impossible to achieve the objective to design, produce and sell 20 units of a product in such a short time span. And in many ways, that is the point. It helps calibrate expectations, both from the potential customers and from the designers. With such little time, customers should not expect premium products and students should not be afraid to make something because the task is too daunting. In addition to the overall calibration, the limited time also has some desired effects on the designer's behaviour.

The time pressure enforces action

The time pressure in this Designerly Entrepreneurship challenge forces an action-first approach, and thus the participants need to revert into acting before (over)thinking. This pushes designers to make sense, situate and use a reflection-in-action approach (Schön, 1983). The desirability bias developed through years of training to be a designer has the side effect that design students tend to become reflection-before-action oriented in their approach. The more they understand the nuances, pitfalls and difficulties of designing, especially in teams, they tend to overthink before they do anything. Thus, the slow down the process in order to minimize the risk of doing the "wrong thing" by trying to analyse what to do. The time pressure forces participants into a reflection in and on action approach.

The sense of urgency drives an effectuation approach

The sense of urgency helps facilitate the students' transition from 'traditional' concept proposal to a more entrepreneurial approach based on effectual actions rather than thinking (Sarasvathy, 2008). With the limited time, you are forced to start with present resources and to engage stakeholders right away. You need to speed up the process and reach out to potential customers simultaneously, as you start sourcing materials, plan the production, etc. Thus, you have to be pragmatic, realistic and quick in the initial research and ideation phase where designers usually spend much time and sometimes become a bit detached from reality. The influence is clear in the product ideas; it avoids unnecessary complexity, detours of wasteful activities and unrealistic elements in the products.

Listen to customer value
We have found that designers' engagement with potential customers is no longer about finding all the things that users would like; instead, it tends to focus more on what creates the biggest value. This limits tendencies, such as feature-creep, the continuous adding of more features to create more perceived value. It also means that designers skip tools like personas, story boards, long discussions and conducting extensive research into identifying the users' problems. They now focus more on defining a clear value proposition for a much simpler product that does not necessarily solve big problems. As an interesting side effect, some designers also 'discover' the power of the aesthetic aspects as part of a value proposition for a product that does not solve new problem, like a wall clock.

Define, design and make 20 units of a product in 10 days, and sell it at Designers' Market.

Why sell at the end?

Facing customers at the end of the process is the driving force of all the other aspects. This provides a powerful element in a development process that can be hard to achieve in reality (especially in an educational setting).
The sales target considers the combination of design and business from the start: "what to design". You need to create and test a value proposition, usually in the form of a concept drawing, mock-up or rendering. Designers engage in a real-world effort to understand what makes their product attractive, but they also continually test how to convince potential customers that their product is relevant.

Beyond pseudo metrics
You are free to choose the type of product. You design your concept, the functionality and aesthetics and determine the amount of money you invest in materials. You choose the complexity of the product, the fit and finish and quality of the material. All this is your choice. But, in the end, you must face the challenge of selling it and ask potential customers for money. This is the key; this is what creates intrinsic motivation (Brabham, 2010). It goes beyond any pseudo metrics. It is the brutal and honest feedback you get, when customers do not buy your product, but go to the 'shop' next to yours to make a purchase.

Clarifying the value proposition
When designers are faced with the challenge to sell, they start looking for desirability, but also for how to attract customers and market the product. Thus, designers must consider the aspects of price, marketing and sales in the product. This means you are now faced with the task of prioritising and communicating the value proposition in a clear, concrete and appealing way. You need to understand what creates customer value, not only user value, and integrate that from the start. This is not just about presenting a value proposition to a third party.

Being the salesperson
At the market event, you find yourself in the position of a salesperson. You now have to actively promote your product and engage in

conversations with total strangers with the objective of making a sale. Prior to the market event, you need to consider the pricing structure and discounts that would make customers want to buy your product and at the same time stay within your budget. With many of the designers we tested this on, we found that people are eager to reach their break-even point in order to get their investment back. Depending on their risk willingness, some have invested more than others, and so they can also potentially can gain more profit. They experience first-hand the relationship between risk and reward.

Why a designerly challenge?

Why a challenge, rather than a process?

In recent years processes like the lean start-up (Ries, 2011) and the google sprint book (Knapp et al., 2016) have gained tremendous success. Process like these acknowledge a death of a pre-planning approaches that need to be replaced with an action-oriented approach, such as build-measure-learn iterations (Ries, 2011) or the quick google sprint of: map, sketch, decide, prototype and test (Knapp et al., 2016). Where the lean start-up helps entrepreneurs with an experimental approach to build a start-up (off-set in a software context), the google sprint book offers teams in (often large) companies a time scheduled approach to working together, aligning and testing ideas.

Both processes lay out a more rapid approach to reducing superfluous work, however they tackle different pains. The lean start-up is essentially about uncertainties, not knowing what and how to calibrate the value proposition to the market to make a scalable business. The process explicitly names and encourages pivots and experiments, driving for rapid learning, adaption, and adjustment (Ries, 2011). Whereas the sprint process solves issues of alignment across stakeholders and focused development time. Through timeboxing mockup and user-test activities, it drives focus and efficiency (Knapp et al., 2016). Both these processes are developed for alignment and clarity of communication in diverse teams (Knapp et al., 2016).

We found that when designers or design students use these processes, they put aside the core of the design profession. The value of process has been connected to the milestone. While we in the first semesters give design students timeboxed processes to teach them methods and tools, the real expertise in the design profession lies in their ability to read and interact with the situation – also described as situated actions (Suchman, 1987). The major truth criterion or value purpose for designers is contextual meaning making both in terms of the process and final solution (Cross 2006; Krippendorff 2006). So instead of prescribing to designers which process steps to take reach to a business end, we flipped the approach.

What makes the challenge designerly?

The challenge is framed within and assumes a designerly paradigm (Laursen and Tollestrup, 2017; Laursen and Haase, 2019). The process is set completely free, but with a challenge that clear is in its framing 'Sell 20 pieces of a product you produced yourself in 10 days'. It draws on designerly methodological approaches, where designers learn through modal shifts, co-evolution of problem and solution, reflective practice and solution led goal analysis exercise their design expertise in a business context.

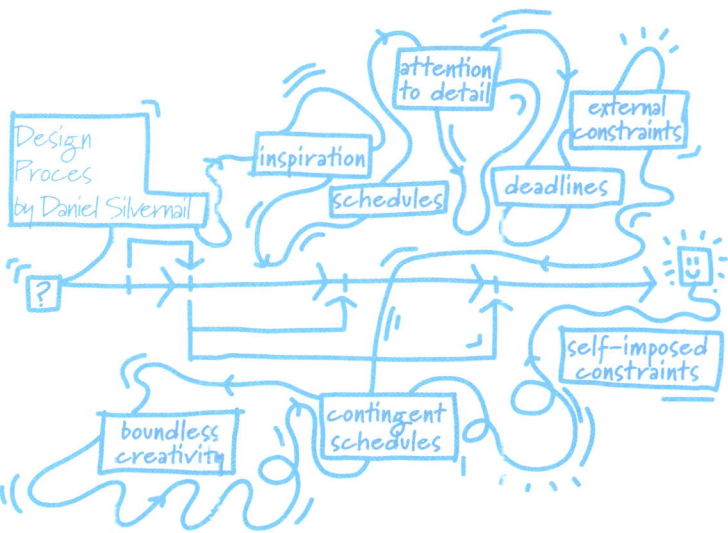

Modal shifts
Through the framing of this challenge, we experienced designers shift modus and take the perspective of the business owners, the producers, the marketers and the designers. Not only as planning, but in a pragmatic resources-seeking-proposal making mode. This is what Sarasvathy (2008) characterised as effectuation. By making designers the owners of all aspects of designing and bringing a product to the market, we push them to take a holistic approach with inevitable modal shifts, where the relation between the resources, production, business and market becomes real. Prior studies show that designers are skilled in rapidly shifting their attention between different tasks, perspectives and types of activities (Akin and Lin, 1995). And these modal shift increase the quality of the final design (Cross 2006). In fact, these modal shifts provide real pragmatic integration and a realistic understanding of the relation between investment, risk, design, production, marketing, sales etc. It facilitates a holistic, but focused product development process that integrates human, business and technology aspects from initial idea to the final sale.

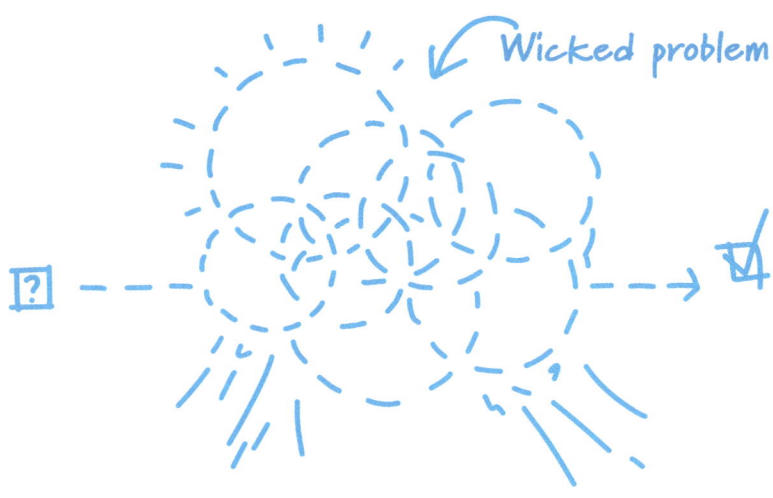

Co-evolution of problems and solutions
The entire setting creates an immersive experience of co-evolution of what a company goes through when developing new products. The challenge feels messy because the problem and the solution co-evolve and are in constant flux, and only action can bring you forward. All aspects co-develop from defining "what to design", setting a budget, developing a concept, sourcing materials and sub suppliers, setting up production, doing the production, ironing out problems, promoting the value proposition, creating the point of sale and selling and making a profit on the product in the market. The participants engage in an iterative process of proposal making and an understanding of the consequences of such proposals, whereby an increased understanding of both the problem and the solution emerges (Dorst and Cross 2001).

The challenge is framed as a wicked problem that, above all, is multifaceted, interdependent, situated, and lacks a singular clear solution and contextually complex (Rittel and Webber, 1973). The tension of the market, production, design, investment, risk etc. are being explored through the solution. You learn about the problem by trying to solve it, which dovetails well with a view of design as a learning process (Schön, 1983; Lawson and Dorst, 2013).

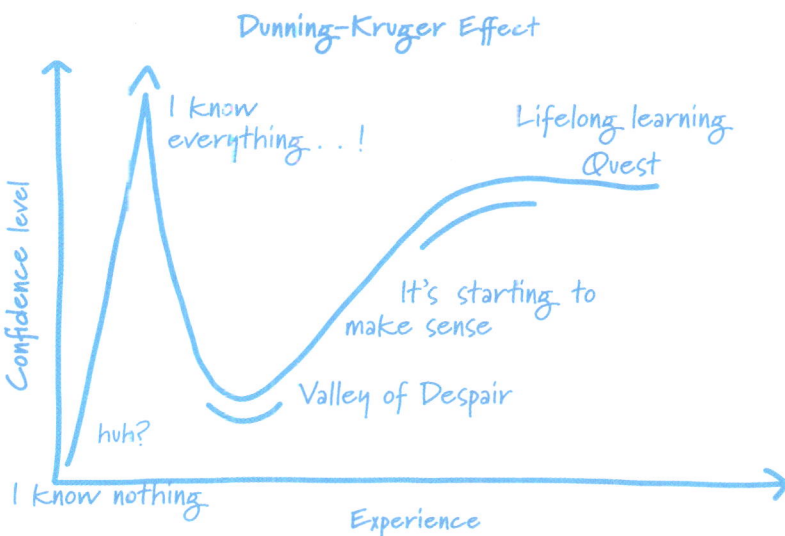

Reflective practice
The time pressure of the challenge forces participants back into an act then reflect approach (Buchanan, 1992). Through our many years of educating designers, we discovered an interesting side effect. As a designer's competence and experience increases, this leads to an increased effort to consider, plan for and arrange the process, methods and procedures in order to take the right path (Lawson, 2019) – a reflection before-action approach. In fact, at some point designers spend most of their time thinking, planning and laying out which actions to take. They invest a large amount of time and effort in pre-argumentation before acting. We find that many designers at a certain competence level are unable to recognise their lack of ability to control and preplan the design process. In order to push them beyond the 'I know it all' stage in the Dunning-Kruger model, we framed this challenge to push the designers to get out of their pre-argumentation and planning mode and take action. Ultimately to take a leap into deep new learning of the context, user, business, technology. etc. (Lawson and Cross, 2013).

Carefully planning and laying out a path to avoid past mistakes do not work in design. This often results in a lower quality design, where designers become fixated on their plan and overlook critical learnings that are key to any design project. Instead, this challenge frames an action-oriented approach that enforces reflection in-action and reflection-on-action (Schön, 1983).

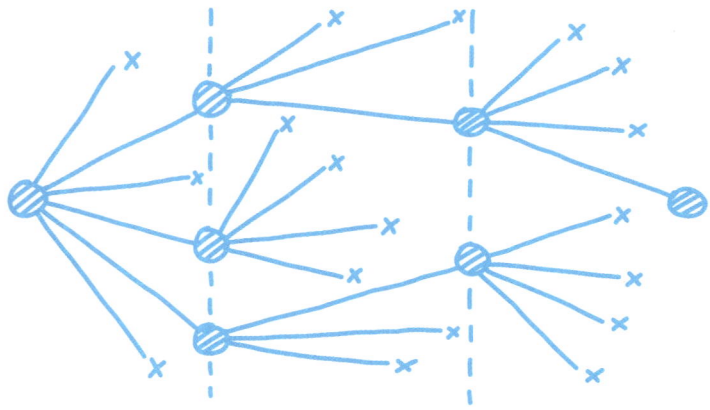

Solution-led goal analysis

The entire setting promotes a more entrepreneurial mindset for designers, advocating for a solution-oriented approach.

You do not focus on what could benefit users through a visionary and divergent concept development process, instead you try to propose product ideas that customers are willing to purchase. This adds a customer-centric approach to product development to the basic user-oriented approach to design and it creates a design-based entrepreneurial approach to business development. The focus is on finding the right solution and ensuring that it is meaningful to the users; the context is a cornerstone of design methodology (Cross, 2006; Krippendorff 2006). However, in this challenge we also now pay more attention to the business side: How does this solution match your own resources, who you know in your network, how much the money you are willing to risk and invest, how many the skills and competences do you have in craftmanship. Therefore, what many perceive as missteps, or starting all over, we do not perceive as failure, but learning about the problem and solution. You cannot restart a design project. It may feel like you must go back and start from scratch. It may seem that you have explored the "wrong part of the map", but you cannot go back to the point where you erase the experience of the things you did, the proposals you tested, the interviews you made. That is now part of your background knowledge about the problem and the potential solution space (Lawson, 2018). You just need to figure out how to use it.

Photo: Quang Tran

The cases

Case Analysis Structure

The cases we studied all have in common that they progress from resources you transform into the ideas that you materialise into 20 units of a product that you promote and sell. Every step involves evaluation and reflection as usual, but when you are the investor, you also include a business case evaluation throughout the process.

Define
What to do? This is the key question in the ideation phase of the process. It is not that different from any other design process, in terms of the approach, methods and tools. What makes this different is the boundaries and limitations related to the resources. At this point, you already start to consider how to make ends meet. What are your resources and who are the customers?
At the end of the process is the sale at the market event, so you start to consider who will attend the market and what sort of products people buy in that situation. You try to balance your available resources with the types of products that people will buy at a market. It is essential to search for something a customer would buy without focusing too much on solving problems and addressing hard needs. This includes early considerations about price range for spontaneous purchases as well as your own decision about how much you are willing to invest in the project. Your risk-willingness and price range are your first business case considerations.

Design
When the idea of a product has taken form, the next step is developing the concept. At the sketching level, there are two main concerns to include in the design.
The first concern is: Will people buy it? Probing the product concept with people adds a dimension of testing the value proposition when interacting with potential customers. At the same time, you are very interested in the different target groups' perception of this value proposition because you have to try to identify a price point.
The second concern is: How do I make it? Sketches or early 3D renderings may seem nice and finished, but they are not detailed, and construction, assembly and production may not have been considered sufficiently. But with the limited time, these considerations become more crucial early in concept development (production dimension).
When the concept becomes more detailed, and you start to consider

the production, the choice of investment vs potential profit becomes very concrete. Sourcing materials may be a large part of the budget, and some processes may require external assistance. At this point, the business case is revisited with concrete estimations on cost, sales price and potential profit.

Make
When you start the actual production process, most decisions on the product have already been made. This does not mean the product development is complete. The aspects you did not consider during the concept development will appear in the production process and require your attention; for example, changes in the design and/or construction. Even if you considered the design for production, there might still be problems and challenges when creating 20 identical pieces. Usually, post-processing activities, such as polishing and assembly, are underestimated.

Sell
When the production is set in motion, more attention is allocated to the promotion and marketing of the soon-to-arrive product. With the focus on the sale at the market, the venue has to be designed and produced. The storytelling about the product needs to be visible at the point of sale. This leads to considerations on how to create attention before and at the market. This may include promotional activities and pre-sale efforts in an attempt to lower the risk of not selling enough during the market event. Ultimately, it ends with a booth or point of sale that displays the product and the value proposition and allows potential customers to see and buy the 20 units.

Case aspects –
The pressure Cooker

This Designerly Entrepreneurship challenge is 'a pressure cooker version' of a product development and go-to-market process. It reduces the entire process down to approximately 10 days. The process from idea to finished product, packaged and displayed and ready for sale, is now confined by four aspects. It is the combination of these four aspects and the time limitation that is core of the challenge. Let us look at these four aspects:

Resources
Resources relate to skills, methods and knowledge about all sorts of topics. When you are put under the pressure of creating 20 units of a self-designed product on your own in 10 days, you suddenly develop a keen interest in what is available. The effectuation approach (Sarasvathy, 2008) of an entrepreneur becomes very relevant. What materials, processes and machines are you most familiar with, and what do you have access to, either yourself or through your network? These aspects represent the elements you can use to create opportunities for product ideas. But they also set some limitations on the quality

and complexity you can deal with within the timeframe. You will start listing your skills, your network (who am I and who do I know?). There is no time to wait, no time to develop new skills, and it does not seem reasonable to start dreaming of creating a product beyond your reach; thus, the vision-oriented approach to ideation in the beginning of the design process changes. It will very quickly become rooted in the resources available or that you can source with short notice, and you are limited by the financial resources you are willing to risk in the project (affordable loss), too.

Production
When you 'own' the entire process from ideation to materialising 20 units of a product, you will also own your own problems and the 'consequences' of your design. There is no longer a company, a production engineer or someone else who will have to transform the product concept into something that can be produced. This puts the design for production aspect right at the centre of your attention. If you ignore this in the conceptualisation phase, you will pay the price later in the production, when you realise you have created too many subcomponents and it takes more time to process. Or you have not considered the assembly procedure or simply not considered post-processing requirements, like polishing.

Production is no longer something you consider at an academic level or as an aspect that you know will have to be dealt with at some point, usually by someone else. It is now a relevant and critical aspect of the design process. So, what are your capabilities? What can you do in the workshop? What processes and tools are you familiar with? How complex is the issue? How challenging is it? How long will it take? What might go wrong? These questions become very decisive for the product concept and production.

Business
The concept of a business case in the Designers' Market context is very simple. It is not about strategies, deliberate loss-products or scalability potential. It could be in a different context, but here it is about selling all 20 units.

Interacting with potential users to get feedback on the product's features, functionality and aesthetics also changes your perspective. You are now interested in understanding whether they are potential customers and whether they are the willing to pay for your product. And if so, how much? You start profiling the relevant customers for your product and consider the price point. With your own money as investment and very little time for execution, you are searching for the most relevant product features that will create value for the potential customer. Limited resources and time automatically challenge the complexity and many of the features. You aim for a clear and concise value proposition (represented by your proposed product; see Österwalder and Pigneur, 2010).

The primary objective is to get your investment back. In other words, to reach the break-even point and preferably do this before the 20 units are sold. The business case is good if you get substantially more out of the venture than you invested. The 'substantially' part is very context dependent. In a learning context, profit is not the main driver; however, with all the uncertainties, reaching the break-even point is a victory.

Market

Bringing the product to market is the objective of all product development. In this case, it is literately a Designers' Market. Taking the product to market means that, during the production phase, you already realise that you need to consider that potential customers need to know about your product. That becomes increasingly relevant when you invest your own money. The notion of marketing a product is not academic and speculative; it is very real and relevant. Having a good product idea is not sufficient; you are very interested in creating awareness of the product, thus engaging in promotional activities prior to going to the Designers' Market.

The ultimate feedback is whether or not you can sell your product. This is part of the main driver of the activities leading up to the market. The marketing and promotion of the product must extend to the sales situation. Staging the point of sale is part of the storytelling and positioning of the product and you as the vendor. You must now actively engage with potential customers who visit the venue and actively promote your product in order to sell it. This is a completely different kind of sales pitch and it becomes very concrete when you ask a person for money for something you have created yourself. The pricing strategy and price point need to balance with your value proposition in a way that will trigger a sale.

pre-sale efforts in an attempt to lower the risk of not selling enough during the market event. Ultimately, it ends with a booth or point of sale that displays the product and the value proposition and allows potential customers to see and buy the 20 units.

The aspects of the pressure cooker
A pressure cooker is a cooking device that helps speed up the process of simmering and tenderising meat, allowing all the flavours in a stew to melt together. Instead of leaving the pot on the stove for hours, you clamp the lid on tightly and it builds pressure that accelerates the natural processes of developing the flavours and tenderising the meat.

Case
The Hanging / Table Lamp

Designer: Line Lundgaard

This case is about a designer's ambition and determination to go all in on the design challenge. It is about carefully testing the value proposition and pricing to ensure the valid business case prior to production. It is also about working relentlessly, gathering additional resources and not lowering the design ambitions when faced with obstacles in the process.

Photo: Sebastian Hougaard Andersen

Define
The designer combined her desire to make a specific product with careful market positioning of the lamp.

The designer's starting point in this challenge was her pre-interest in and desire to design a lamp.

After settling on the product type, the designer employed a bird-in-the hand principle to resolve the production method early on, asking questions such as: What do I know? and What do I have access to? In order to reduce uncertainty and risk, it was important to settle on a production method that was within her skillset. As the designer previously had worked with a laser cutter and had access to one, she settled on that approach.

Thus, contrary to conventional design processes, the guiding principle included a combination of a pre-chosen product category and a production method. This meant that the designer could narrow down the solution space very quickly.

"I wanted to show my design ability. What I could do on my own. While it was also fear-provoking, this was my chance to realise a design myself.

Design
User probing used to decide on the style in detail and to adhere to high design standards and ambitions provides a clear value proposition with embedded values of a long-lasting product.

The designer initiated the process with an ideation sketching session. Since the production method was defined (laser cutting), the solution space was quickly scoped as a slated lamp concept, which, at the time, was very popular. In order to differentiate the product in the market, the design developed into it not only being a one-purpose lamp, but a lamp designed for multiple situations, such as hanging over a table, in a corner or standing on a table.

From the user probing, the price was set at 250 DKK (90 DKK overhead), and the design was tweaked a bit. Initially, the investment of the designer was set to a 1,000 DKK, but the user research provided such confidence-inspiring feedback that she decided to use better materials. She upgraded the choice of wood and used a cord with fabric wrapping. She even made bespoke packaging with her brand on it. Ultimately, she increased the investment in the product to 3,000 DKK.

The upgrade in materials also fit with the designer's ambition of making a product that would last and creating something she was proud of. From this point on, she had a clear focus on maintaining high standards.

> *I think I spent 1/3 of the time sketching, and then I spent a huge amount of time doing cardboard models, where I cut out the slates and assembled them in different ways. I think I made seven different versions in cardboard that I also used to ask different target groups regarding desirability, price, aesthetics.*

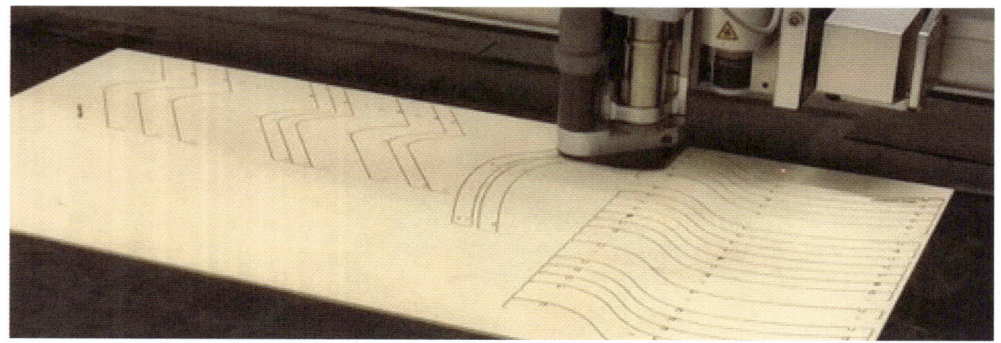

Make
Setting a high standard meant that the designer needed to network for manufacturing labour to make up for underestimating the time and effort in post-processing.

Five days into the 10-day time frame, the production process started. Cutting the slates using the laser cutter was fairly straight forward. The only concern was placing the cut-outs to maximise the use of the sheet and not waste materials.

However, the designer was somewhat surprised by the post-processing requirements. In order to achieve the desired surfaced quality, the slates required additional treatment. Manually sanding, oiling and assembling the 400 wood slates and the 60 wood circles connecting the slates was extremely time-consuming. So, she enlisted help from her network to be able to finish in time.

> I think I underestimated the time it took. By the end of the process, I asked my friend and boyfriend to help me with the manual after treatment. It was a big task being on my own.

Despite being under time pressure, the designer decided to make custom packaging. Again, she used the bird-in-the-hand strategy and reached out to people in her network.

> I had a friend that gave a helping hand in the process. She got a lamp in return. She had a connection in her network that made print on fabric. So, I got to borrow the machine and we had sewn custom-made fabric bags for the lamp. I am of the conviction that you will attain whatever you set yourself to.

Sell
The designer used a comprehensive marketing and promotion strategy at the point of sale, including branded packaging. This thought-through storytelling caters to different customer profiles and needs.

The designer made an effort to visually communicate the potential use of the product at the actual market. Displaying three to four ways of using the product in a home, she tried catering to different customer profiles and needs.

I displayed them with different light bulbs where with slated lamps the bulb is directly visible, right. So, the light might blind people; therefore, it might not provide the best lightning. It is more of a design element.

She displayed the different ways the product could be used, and she styled it to fit various homes. There were different colours of fabric cords and different colours of the rubber band that holds the lamp together. The market booth consisted of a hanger with four different lamps, each with a different light bulb, as well as a night table upon which a lamp was standing.

The intent was to show off different situations where you could use the lamp. So, people could understand that it was multipurpose; it could adapt to different situations in the home.

Photo: Sebastian Hougaard Andersen

Key Take Away

Let us look at what was significant in this lamp case. What did the designer do successfully, and what did she neglect, ignore or not prioritise?

In this case, the designer employed a strong design strategy at the beginning of the process, and she made a passion-driven choice of product and had high ambitions for the quality of the materials and finish. The thorough feedback on value proposition through various design variations supported her decision to increase the price point and generate interest in the product. In turn, this was used to allocate more resources to the materials and product quality. This designer integrated the business and design before acknowledging the consequences for the production. This meant additional resources were required to deliver the desired quality and quantity. The designer followed through by displaying the product and its adaptability to customers' homes at the point of sale. The focus on risk in the design (quality) and business (value proposition) led to a blind spot for the production risks.

• • • • • • • • • • • • • •

Succes
The designer had a very strong focus on delivering a high-quality product that successfully sold out before the market ended. The result was a high level of consistency in value in the product with keen attention to product details, quality and desirability for customers.

Compromise
Not much effort went into foreseeing the consequences of the design in terms of production time and especially the post-production processing of the components. The cost was that the designer had to spend her spare time doing the work and she had to increase production capacity by enlisting her friends as her manual labour force.

Learning
The designer proved that it was possible to maintain a high standard for the design, but that came at a price in terms of the lack of (own) resources in the production.

The designer's own key take-away
Line Lundgaard's take-away was: "It was a tremendous success to experience setting the bar very high and still supersede the target". She still designs and makes new lamps in her spare time.

Calibrating the level of ambition: *Resources vs Production*

By relating the available resources with your production capabilities, you set the level of ambition for the product to be created. On the one hand, you have access to your skills, resources, materials and network, which is what is available. You then combine this with your knowledge and access to tools, machines and manufacturing processes, and you define the capabilities. The number of resources you allocate for the project and the extent to which you leverage your manufacturing capabilities are defined by your ambition and your risk willingness.

Are you staying within your comfort zone, only engaging in manufacturing processes, materials and techniques you are already familiar with and thus within your skill set (resources)?

Or are you trying to raise the bar, so you need to expand your resources and enlist assistance to complete some of the processes?

Case
The Wall Cushions

Designers: Anton Malmkjær Møller & Quang Tran

This case is about continually testing the value proposition to prove the business viability before committing to an investment. Moving from top-down targeting to a bottom-up strategy, leveraging one's own resources, skills, know-how and insights proved to be successful.

Define

A 'top-down' imitation strategy of a perceived hyped product failed through value proposition testing. The team needs to pivot.

The design team had a feeling that this project needed to start at full speed because of the short timeline. The designers wanted to do something that, effort-wise, was easy and low budget, but through their creativity, they would be able to infuse value and earn money. Hence, the main focus for the designers was to create a viable business case.

Design-wise, they wanted to tap into the larger do-it-yourself (DIY) trend that was trending at that moment. They went on Pinterest and quickly found examples of PU-foam-DIY vases. It met their criteria of being a 'designer-product' that was easy and cheap to produce, while possibly being sold at a higher mark-up.

"
Shit, what a task. How are we ever going to reach that? And are we ever going to sleep the next few weeks?

"
Our mantra was: fail fast, fail early, fail forward.

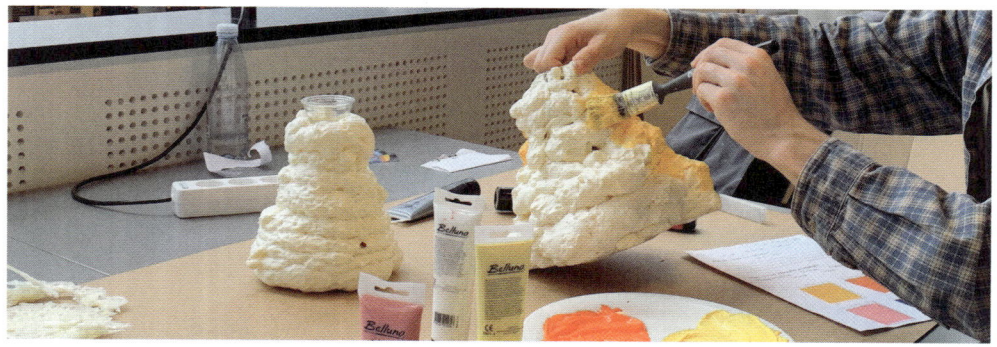

As the designers wanted to ensure their product was attractive, they went to great lengths to examine and verify the customer interest. So, they decided to conduct a user-desirability test on Instagram. They posted digital stories on Instagram asking viewers to share their opinions through votes. Practically, they found photos in environments and posted them on Instagram as stories with the text:

- 'Check out this cool vase.'
- 'Perfect for the personal and unique interior.'
- 'Could you imagine this vase in your home?'
- 'Yes/no'

Of the people that responded, 92% answered No; among the 8% of the people who responded Yes were the designers themselves. In addition to the Instagram test, they made a physical prototype, which they followed up with an analogue questionnaire. Based on the prototype and the user feedback, they realised that they would spend almost as much in materials as they could charge to sell the product; thus, consumers did not expect a high price point.

There were a couple of girls that said we could make that for 20 DKK with materials from the shop. We came to close to something people could make themselves.

This left the designers with no choice but to rethink what product they could make.

Design
The designers used the bird-in-the hand strategy to leverage their insights, skills, resources and experience to focus on execution. The team proved the new product's business potential by pre-selling units prior to their commitment to production.

Having wasted a couple of days on the vase idea, the design team quickly reframed the design process, this time taking a bottom-up approach. Using Sarasvathy's (2008) bird-in-the hand strategy, the designers looked for skills, resources and insights that they already possessed.

One of the designers identified an older design project with wall cushions that he had made, which he remembered there being a pretty high demand for. He activated the Facebook marketplace ad for selling the wall cushions again; and he wrote to previously interested customers who had left empty-handed.

They quickly got feedback. Between 60–70% of the previous customers replied the same day that they were still interested in the product at a price of 400 DKK. The designers were already familiar with the construction and production methods. Therefore, most of their work became validating the business case before even starting the design project. Before production, 5–10 units were already pre-ordered. The design process was a proof of business, where the value proposition for the design was tested and 'pre-purchases' were made prior to committing to production

We weren't going to just stand there at the market, and people were not going to buy our product. We simply weren't ready to take that risk.

Make

Using their know-how on pillow manufacturing and leveraging access to materials and expert tools kept costs down and sped up of the process. Prototyping for manufacturing and careful planning limit the waste of time and materials.

Another member of the design team leveraged his network resources. Through a family member he had access to high quality foam and Kvadrant fabric. With the designers' previous experience in making the wall pillows, they knew the foam cutting part was crucial, time-consuming and difficult to get right by hand. So, they actually ensured that the cold foam was cut at the factory.

The production was straight forward for them. Since they had previous experience with this product, they knew where the pitfalls were. They first made a prototype and planned the setup from that. They made patterns for the fabric and found the size for the wood sheets. In that way, they tested the manufacturing process before scaling the production to all of the 20 units.

With the entire production planned, the actual manufacturing took as little time as possible. They cut all the fabric, MDF sheets and then they finally assembled the pillows.

It is kind of like pancakes; the first one became a bit ugly. But then we knew how much fabric we needed. Then we could cut out 20 pieces of fabric at once.

Sell
The designers relied on customer profiling using Facebook Marketplace interaction to identify the type of customer and price point. They focused their marketing effort on increasing awareness and ensuring a high success rate.

With a smooth and well-planned manufacturing process, they finished the production of all 20 pillows two days before the actual market. That left plenty of time to build a booth for the market.

To further strengthen the promotion of their product, they also developed a marketing plan to create awareness and get more customers to the market to buy the other half of their products.

They collected money from all the groups to make collective targeted Facebook ads inviting people to this event.

In the end, they did not solely rely on selling their pillows at the market. They pre-sold a little over 50% of their pieces before the market through Facebook Marketplace. Thus, they were confident that they already had a working sales channel that eventually would help them sell out all 20 pieces.

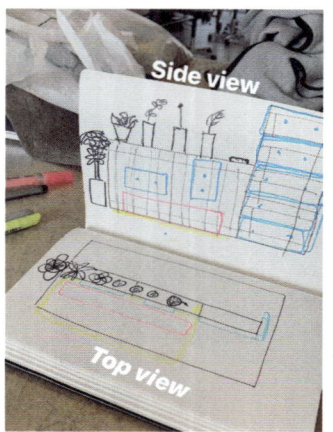  

❝
We started this booth in the middle of the design studio, while all the other teams where still doing their products. And it set off a chain reaction, where everyone started to build a booth.

❝
We did a Facebook event. Did photos and posts on our own and the others' products, to enhance the entire market success. We wrote to the local newspaper. Made signs and banners. The PR and marketing effort were tremendous.

Key Take Away

Let us look at what was significant in this wall cushion case. What did the designers do successfully and what did they neglect, ignore or not prioritise? What did they learn from this challenge?

Most of the energy and attention went towards developing the market and identifying potential customers for the product. The aim was to make a good business case and leveraging their resources and network.

By making the designer the investor, this team changed its approach 180 degrees from working with developing a design to developing a business and a market. The team did not spend time and resources on developing a design or concept. Instead, the designers used their resources to streamline production and get a commitment from potential customers (developing the market). The team tried to minimise risk in two ways. Financial risk was addressed by the team's promotional effort. To minimise uncertainties in production, the team re-used an already designed product.

● ● ● ● ● ● ● ● ● ● ● ● ● ● ● ●

Succes
The team successfully sold its products before and after the market, primarily because the designers had the time and skills to scale the promotion and sales effort. This was also possible because they, in principle, scaled a product they had run before with a positive outcome.

Compromise
There was no design, concept development or innovation on the product side. If the team had been a company, the members would not have hired a designer because they saw no need for that service.

Learning
The team proved that it could move beyond the scope of a designer and embrace the production aspect and, most significantly, the market aspect. But it was at the expense of design; it was not an integrated approach.

The designer's own key take-away
Anton thought that the biggest learning point was that "you should be ready to act swiftly and change direction if necessary". Quang pointed out the impact of knowing the sales channels and marketing tools.

Finding the idea: *Resources vs Market*

The first tension relates to the beginning: what kind of product should be made? With the limited time and the unknown customer-base at the market, there is a tension between the available resources and the uncertainty of the customer. The ideation may be based on the resources and knowledge available, but it does not provide any reassurance about the relevance of the product to the customers at the market. Throughout the process, there will be a constant flux between the idea and the product and the potential customers using sketches, 3D renderings and 3D models to get feedback on the product proposals. This presents an opportunity to learn about the customer profile relevant for the proposed product. But until a sale has been made, you cannot conclude that the person was a customer and not just a random person.

Case
Hydroponic Pots

Designers: Peter Byrial Jensen & Sebastian Hougaard Andersen

This case is about integrating the designers' personal interests, skills and passion to create a successful product. The design team considered and prioritised manufacturing and materials beyond the shaping (and then functionality) when conceptualising the product to manage the risk during the process. At the end, the team worked with an exhibition-fish pot to create awareness and attract customers.

Define
The designers first identified an impulse-buy product and price point for customers at the venue. They used materials as part of defining the product.

This was the first time the design team had to design a product that they also needed to produce and sell.

We were yearning for projects that were real. We were working on projects with companies, but now we actually needed to reach an end-customer for real. Not just a prototype, but an alpha model, ready to the market. It was really engaging to have such a fast process. Being pressured to do it.

The team started the design process as usual, with a sketching process putting ideas to paper. The scoping into a specific product type happened fairly quickly, based on the type of customers the team expected to be present at the market and the purchase situation. Since the market was a one-time Designers' Market, the team guessed that people would not go there to buy something specific. Rather, purchasing would be more of a spontaneous impulsive decision. Based on that, the team's rationale was based on what type of products people would buy on impulse and what price points would induce people to make an impulse buy? Based on their own experience as students, since the venue was on campus, the designers decided on a DDK 50 price point.

The specific product type, self-watering pots, was based on the personal interest of the design team. The designers were fascinated by hydroponic pots, which they considered to be a tiny ecosystem. Their first idea was to make biomes that were self-sufficient, where a fish could live off the plant and the plant could live off the fish. However, realising that this was unrealistic, they proceeded with the self-watering pots leaving the fish behind…for a while.

To define the scale of the investment and to calibrate their common understanding of the risk, they used Sarasvathy's (2008) affordable loss principle and agreed to invest DKK 1,000 in the project. If they lost it all that would be okay.

Design
The team used manufacturing capabilities to guide the design decisions and used available materials and interest in resin as an integrated part of the design.

In the next step, the designers started by making prototypes in clay, but quickly realised that this production method did not work well. The finish was not acceptable, and the manufacturing method was not suitable for making a large batch of 20 products.

The production aspect, we tried to consider that from the beginning and lots of other stuff. In regular design projects, we didn't have to consider all of these many aspects simultaneously; but in this project, it felt like we might kill the entire project on one mistake, so we had to consider it.

The design team looked at materials that could be developed to ensure a great finish. The designers found acrylic tubes to be sharp, round and smooth, so they bought these tubes and used them as the main component. Other materials were chosen based on the design team's skills and passion. One of the designers loved to work in wood, and another had a fascination with resin, which is a type of plastic that dries and becomes transparent.

We wanted to make something with a great finish and were pretty aware of our own lack of talent in shaping something by hand.

The designers quickly made a 3D model of the aspired product, within day 3.

Make
The team carefully planned and prepared a production pipeline and setup to minimise errors and reduce the amount of time and materials needed for production.

The purchased materials were relatively expensive; they included mahogany wood, acrylics tubes and resin from a boat maker. Even though the wood was something one of the designers had laying around, the design team was aware of the value of the materials. The aspiration was to make it look like a mass-produced product.

Unfortunately, the design team experienced snags in the production. When the designers started to cut the first acrylic tube on a band saw, it splintered. Acrylic is a hard and crisp material. It became obvious that they needed to be careful with their inventory

of materials. They did not have enough acrylic to keep risking splintering half of the tubes. That meant putting more work into preparing the manufacturing process. They printed a 3D shape that they used as a template. That enabled them to shape the tube gradually (without splintering) at the sanding belt.

hey also built a makeshift lathe to shape the wood block, using an electric drill at the one end and a nail on the other end of the wooden leg. Thus, the design team spent time carefully planning and setting up the steps in the production. The subsequent manufacturing of the parts happened fairly quickly.

With the two main components ready, the top acrylic part and the bottom wood part were assembled using the resin. This happened around day 9. Later, the team discovered that several of the pots were leaking; something had happened to the resin, or maybe the resin did not bind well on a smooth surface. The designers had to reapply resin, adding extra time to the process.

Sell

The designers promoted their product through storytelling and a gimmick (fish) to create attention and awareness. They used consistent follow-up at the market by carefully considering their competitors at the sales venue and clearly differentiating their marketing material.

The team realised that it was difficult to create awareness of its product. Even during the design process, when the team members had asked people whether they would purchase the product, they learned that it was difficult to bring attention to the product. So, they started asking: How do we get people's attention?

> *So, we were thinking. How do we, when positioned among 10-15 other booths, get people's attention? How do we get them to come over to us? Because they remember us?*

The team circled back to its original crazy idea of including a fish with the plant. The designers had bought additional material, so they could make a larger version of the pot and put a fish in it to create attention and generate discussion about the product. Days before the event, they placed it in the venue building as an eye-catching feature to create awareness. It worked; they now were referred to as 'the ones with the fish'.

Considering their booth design, they found most of the other design teams were working "on the ground" level. They used tables or tried to occupy as much "ground" as possible. So, in order to differentiate themselves, they built a very tall booth of sheets of wooden. The pots were displayed hanging on the sheets so they would be noticed and, to some extent, mimic a showroom.

Likewise, the pricing was based on positioning the products by looking at the competition. They looked at other comparable design teams to understand their prices and they matched their prices accordingly. The final production price was DKK 50 per item, and they sold 1 for DKK 200 and 2 for DKK 300. All the pieces were sold during the market, even the big pot with the fish.

Key Take Away

Let us look at what was significant in this hydroponic case. What did the designers do successfully and what did they neglect, ignore or not prioritize?

Most of the energy and attention went towards planning for and preparing the production of the product. With high-end materials, managing the risk of waste due to failure was a priority. The secondary focus for the team was the marketing efforts to create awareness of the product, both before and during the Designers' market. Creating awareness and differentiating themselves from the competition was important.

The team's pre-choice of materials left little room for exploratory design and product development, and the product category followed a pre-defined trend. The team's pricing strategy was to aim for spontaneous shopping at the market venue and position the product relative to its competitors.

● ● ● ● ● ● ● ● ● ● ● ● ●

Succes
The team successfully sold its products at the market. The designers' promotional strategy before and during the market helped attract attention. The large focus on preparing for production paid off and shortened the amount of time spent producing the 20 units.

Compromise
Not much effort went into the product type and the design. The choice of materials, based on passion, interest and availability, proved to be challenging in terms of durability. The pot was not waterproof.

Learning
The team proved that allocating resources to plan production was time well spent and that their marketing and promotional efforts paid off. The designers managed to integrate production with business and design.

The designer's own key take-away
Peter pointed out that this challenge "does not provide new tools, but allows you to hone the tools you already have and prove that they actually work".
Now knowing that the event of doing a Designers' Market worked, Sebastian would have invested more money. In general, he noted: "It is a confidence booster knowing that you can make products that people will buy."

Telling the story: *Business vs Market*

It is not enough to have made the product, the customer needs to be made aware that it exists and understand its value. Thus, there is a need to engage in promotional activities without having a thorough understanding of who the target groups are and how to address them. There may be tension between the ability to communicate visually, verbally and through products and the potential customers' ability to understand and find the value proposition attractive.

Are you able to precisely create and communicate the value proposition to attract and sell the product to the customer and make it a viable business with a sound business case?

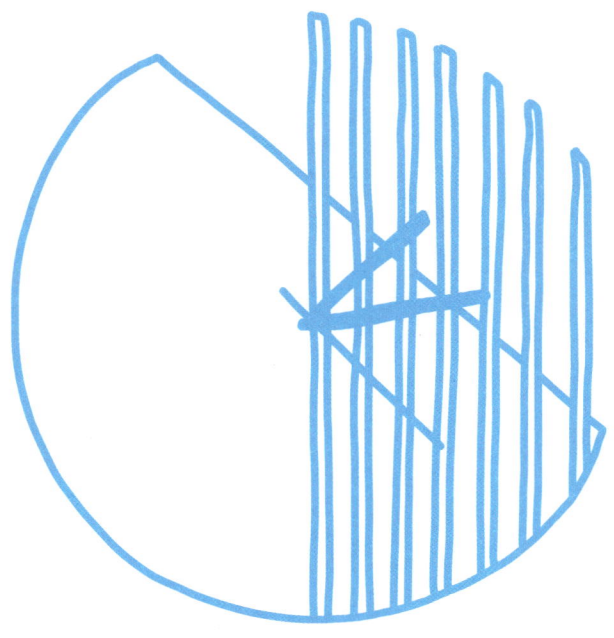

Case
The Wall Clock

Designers: Anne Nold Jensen & Martin Lundberg

This case is about using your gut feeling and listening to the customers. Moreover, when realising the impact not considering the manufacturing aspects had on production time and quality and finish of the product, the designers used the lemonade principle to turn a lack of consistency into a 'hand-made' brand using videos and storytelling to succeed anyway.

Define
The designers defined their skill set and used the available machines to narrow down their solution space. The product category was based on what people buy more than once.

The starting point for this team was the designers' manufacturing skills. Being very aware of their weaknesses in production, they were determined to reduce uncertainty in the process. Therefore, they settled on a production method they were already familiar with. Of all the machines in the workshop they felt most comfortable with the milling machine. They had previous experience working with wood and milling. That part was settled on the first day.

With the main manufacturing method chosen, they started looking into which type of products people always have in their homes and what kind of product they would purchase, even if they already had one.

We kind of skipped the market research on the first iteration and went with our gut feeling: the wall clock is the right product. We both didn't have a wall clock in our home.

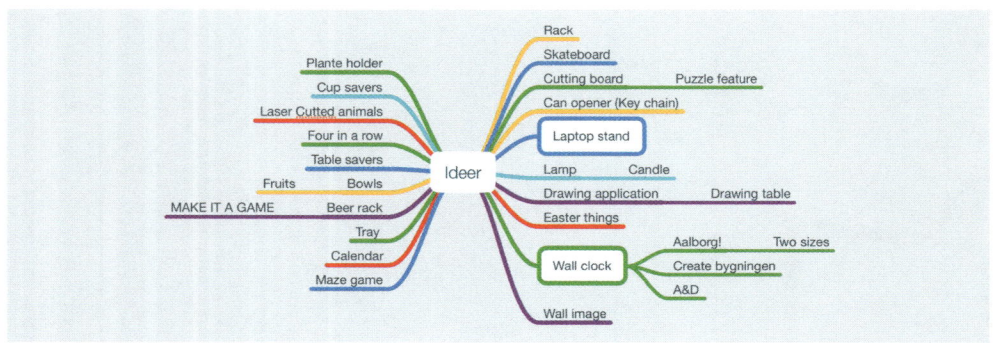

Design

Exploring the value proposition helped the team profile the customers and understand who appreciated the aesthetic value of the product being sold.

Based on the wall clock category, the team still needed a direction for detailing the design. Using Pinterest as a source of inspiration, the designers decided on a Scandinavian style clock.

As part of the product development, they started to look into a personalisation of the wall clock. What if you could place a photo on it, and customise it? The design team did sketches by hand, created prototypes and quick renderings to show the design proposal to random people in the campus building.

The 10 days provoked us to make really fast decisions—based on gut our feeling. If one of us said no, or thought it was wrong, we dropped it immediately.

The feedback made the designers realise that their design was too cluttered. They decided to try to remove the customised photo but keep the small slates that had received positive comments. To confirm their choices and further develop the aesthetics, they revisited the design of

the slates, did new 3D renderings and contacted people again to get feedback. At the same time, they were able to identify a pattern in the feedback. Fellow design and architecture students were less impressed and rated their proposal as having a low value. The students' main argument was that they could have made the clock themselves. Students from the humanities were more positive and placed a higher value on the aesthetics, and they were willing to pay more, close to DKK 200. Thus, the value proposition of a Scandinavian style wall clock made more sense and presented more value to someone not capable of creating aesthetically pleasing products themselves.

Make

Realising and producing a product with a 3D finish proved extremely challenging, and the act of design-for-manufacturing produced less consistent units.

With the renderings from the SolidWorks model in hand and the laser cutter and milling cutter set available, the first part of the production process was supposed to be straight forward. However, since the designers focused on the business case by looking at keeping costs down, they had sourced the wood material to be as affordable as possible. That material required some post-processing steps to live up to the quality of the finish promised by the rendering that was shown to potential customers.

The inexpensive wood required many hours of sanding and paint after the components were cut. In was a tremendous effort to come close to looking like the rendering. Approximately 5 days were spent sanding the components.

Moreover, some of the thin slates proved harder to assemble with the main body than anticipated, mainly due to short overlaps between the components. At this point in the process, it was too late to change the design to align with the assembly method (gluing), and changing the assembly method would compromise the entire design.

At the end of manufacturing, the finish of the product was not as expected.

It was quite challenging to go from render to reality.

Sell
The designers cleverly turned the lack of consistency in the units into a promotional video on handcrafted products.

The designers ended up with 20 pieces of a product not living up to their own expectations despite the many hours of post-processing. What would potential customers think? Offering this product with minor flaws and a less than desired quality of finish at the market presented a challenge.

Using Sarasvathy's (2008) lemonade principle, they decided to turn the 'mistake' into an advantage. During the manufacturing, they decided to make video recordings of the manual manufacturing process. This could now be edited into a "how-it-was-made" movie, showing off female hands gently sanding each of the slates and the clock base. In that way, the minor differences between the clocks and the unintended handmade expression were used in the storytelling and marketed as a strength.

Key Take Away

Let us look at what was significant in the wall clock case. What did the designers do successfully and what did they neglect, ignore or not prioritise?

In testing the value proposition, the focus was on creating value through the product aesthetics for potential customers. However, a strong need for risk management drove the team members to choose inexpensive materials. They did not adjust the design to accommodate the production or the cheaper materials leaving them with a product quality that was lower than that promised by the 3D renderings they had shown to potential customers.

With a compromised quality of material and finish of the final product, they managed to pivot by changing the value proposition and storytelling around the product.

● ● ● ● ● ● ● ● ● ● ● ● ●

Succes
The designers successfully adapted to surprises in the process and created storytelling with videos about the manual production process. This served as an integral part of the sales pitch at the venue, almost creating an automatic salesperson telling the story behind the product.

Compromise
With a conservative approach to risk management as cost reduction, the outcome of production suffered in quality and finish.

Learning
The key take-away is that if development of a new product does not consider the production processes, the product will suffer. And with limited budgets and a conservative risk profile, it is very hard to create new, functioning designs for products.

The designer's own key take-away
Martin said: "We had our focus on break-even, but we should have sacrificed more … and invested in a product we were proud of." He summarised this as: "The more you risk, the greater it gets; but obviously it is also more anxiety provoking."
- Anne's take-away was the power of storytelling and the act of selling in a fair-like setup. "I've used my experience with building up an exhibition at a fair. Like how do you attract people? What story are you conveying?"

Delivering the promise: *Business vs Production*

Promoting the proposed product and trying to validate the value proposition using sketches, and especially 3D renderings, create high expectations. Not only will the potential customers respond to what they perceive as high quality when estimating prices, but the designer costumer might also expect the finished product to look similarly well made. The question is: Are you able to deliver on the promise?

There is a risk of overselling the product in the renderings, but not being able to achieve the expected fit and finish when manufacturing it.

Case
Table Lamp 1

Designers: Anders Miltersen & Palle Høygaard-Jørgensen

This case is about the determination to keep a high design quality that requires the drive to reach out to suppliers to source the needed expertise. It is also a story about engaging suppliers and networks as co-sponsors of the project, leveraging their competencies and resources to drive the project forward.

Define
By copying successful products in order to identify a promising product category for the market and doing their own design using key skills, the designers were able to access resources and prior experience.

The starting point for this design process was the identification of production skills and the designers' fascination with a new software program for 3D printing. One of the designers had prior experience with and was skilled in using the laser cutter. That—combined with the design team's recent fascination with a software program 'slicer' for 3D printing where you upload a shape that the program then slices into 2D shapes that you can then laser cut—became the basis for the ideation.

The design team had an underlying requirement that the production and craftsmanship needed to stretch beyond what anyone could do on their own at home.

The design team wanted to get the most out of the challenge. They thought of it as a unique chance to do the best possible design, and to get the most out of the 10 days, so they decided to invest DKK 2–2,500 per person in the challenge. The investment also increased the amount of energy they invested and their engagement in the project.

> *We started by taking iconic buildings and then iconic design furniture and taking 3D models and slicing them up in a program. Beyond wrestling with getting permission from these brands, we also dropped that idea because it was too easy. We didn't challenge ourselves design wise.*

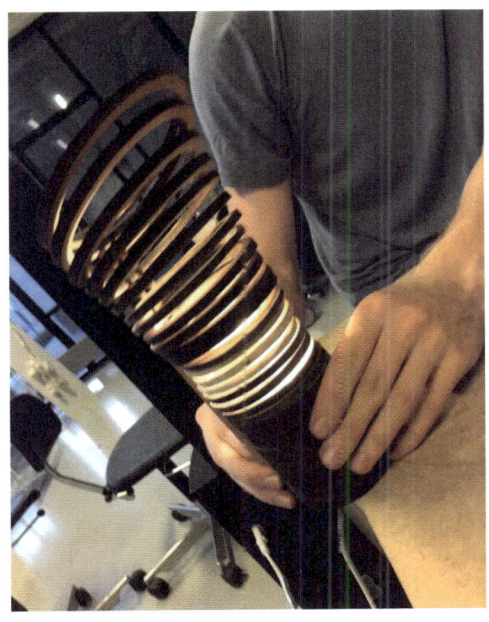

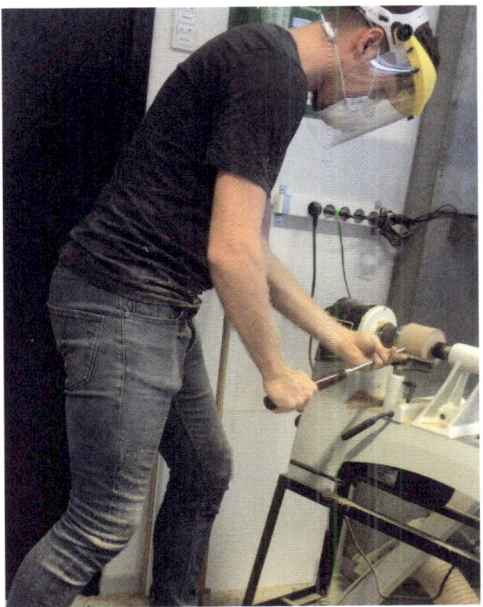

Design
Transferring the slicing approach to a lamp creates appealing aesthetics with surprisingly high value for the customers.

After having worked with miniature buildings and furniture, the design team decided to take a step back and make a 'classic design iteration'. They asked: How can we reuse some of the work when the proposed solution does not work?

The team pivoted to the Milter Sen classic product design category, the lamp. One of the designers had previous experience designing lamps. The other designer always wanted to make a lamp. They also knew that a year earlier, the previous class had designed lamps, and it was a successful category for customers.

They reused the "slicing an object" approach and developed a cylinder shape in 3D with continuous changing geometry from top to bottom. They sliced it and used the 3D rendering to ask potential customers for feedback.

And then we actually realised that the lamp had more value than we thought. Based on other products sold in previous years, we thought we could price it to be around 150 DKK, but people were telling us it was worth about DKK300–400. One even said DKK 800. We realised it was pretty elegant.

After receiving positive feedback, the team sped up the process. The designers went into the workshop to make a prototype to test if the concept could be made into a physical product. They encountered different problems.

Firstly, the base was made in solid oak, but the oak was so hard that it created many problems in the lathe. That was not the only problem. The birchwood rings got a black line on the edge and partly on the surface from the cutting process (burning). It needed a lot of post-process sanding that the team had to consider when planning the production. However, the most difficult thing was the spine of the product.

> *The spine that holds the rings together; we started making that in a 20x20 cm wood profile, where with a circular saw, we did the slots, which the rings were supposed to be inserted into. However, while they are horizontal on the bottom, further up they have a little angle that gives the dynamic and elegant design expression, and that was extremely difficult to achieve. Then, we had to think about alternatives.*

In the process of making a prototype of the product and using the intended production methods, the designers realised that they had to rethink their approach to production. They simply could not achieve the desired product quality.

Make
The designers leveraged their network for sourcing the right competencies for a key process and engaged suppliers as co-sponsors to minimise their cost while increasing the quality of their product.

The wooden spine was impossible to make with any acceptable level of precision. They needed a stronger material and decided to make it from steel. But they could not do that themselves, so they started to look for help from others with expertise in laser-cutting steel.

We talked with many people that had capabilities within laser-cutting steel. But it was difficult. Nobody could do it. Not in the way we wanted anyway. It was important for us that the angles increase gradually and be quite precise, because that kind of gives the entire expression in the lamp.

The designers learned that laser-cutting steel to produce a lamp was very difficult, because it was not as trivial as laser cutting something that is flat. You need to laser to cut a tube with a square profile and twist it in the process.

The first call went to a family member, but the profiles where too small for their machines. Then, the designers called a teacher at a technical school, but he was not allowed to help them. Both designers simultaneously called people to source capabilities, and in the end they found BLT (Beritech).

> *We first got a price of DKK 65. per spine. That turned out to be a lot compared to the sales price we expected. Then we talked a bit with him and got the idea that we could maybe offer publicity at the market, where a lot of designers would be present. We could place their brochure and show them off as a sponsor. And he agreed but requested that we bring three Othello layered cakes."*

BLT saw this sponsorship as an investment. If the prototype batch was successful, it might lead to further sales. Thus, more spines would need to be cut. BLT became a stakeholder and co-owner in the project. But this was not the only business decision they made in order to cut costs without sacrificing quality. The base was an oak plank that was sourced from of the father of one of the designers. The lamp socket was sourced from IKEA with an employee discount, because one of the designers worked there.

The birch wood for the rings was also sourced without a direct financial transaction. At first, they got a price from the workshop at the university. But inspired by their initial success with the steel spine, they tried to find a sponsor for the wood. In the end, they found a company, Keflico, to sponsor the birch wood. They even managed to get the workshop staff at the university to help with the actual transportation to the workshop.

In the process of cutting the rings out of the wooden sheets, the design team tried to optimise the use of material to get as many rings as possible from each sheet of wood. The designers had to revisit the design; they shrunk the four bottom rings and increased the four top rings, so these would fit within each other, thus minimising material waste

Sell

The designers used a network to launch a call-to-action with renderings and pre-sales to customers before attending the market. They followed through on the value proposition in the sales situation and cared for the customer experience, but they failed to dare to ask the right price.

Right after the designers had created a 3D rendering, they started to test the market for the product. They put it on web page of the online shop of the mother of one of the designers. It was advertised as a "sold out" product that you could sign up for. They wanted to understand the demand at different price ranges, and they were surprised that customers were willing to pay DKK600 for the lamp.

So, we wanted to finish it before the market, so we knew how many we had left. We sold 4 on the web shop in a couple of days and had 16 left for the market.

To be able to ship the lamp, the design team developed packaging for the product. The designers had cardboard boxes sponsored by the mother of one of the designers (the one with a web shop) and they printed a label to place on the box.

At the market, the designers built an "exhibition" using white cubes with a product in each box. All the products were sold out in 15 minutes, at a price of DKK 295. each. In the end, the demand was so high that they started making a list for additional customers to sign up.

Key Take Away

Let us look at what was significant in this table lamp case. What did the designers do successfully and what did their neglect, ignore or not prioritise?

Once the team members pivoted to the lamp, they managed to combine the production technology of slicing with the design and aesthetics of the lamp. Using a call-to-action method to test the price and interest in the product, they also integrated and maintained a business perspective throughout the process. The online platform provided feedback and an opportunity to create a pre-sale situation. The designers were determined to maintain their aesthetic value proposition in the built quality of the lamp. This led to a combination of the clever use of suppliers for the most critical component and the less clever choices of processes for production that required many hours of post-processing. In the end, this led to a significant improvement in the business case.

• • • • • • • • • • • • • • •

Succes
The designers had the ability to follow through on the design quality in the production by sourcing expertise to build the most critical components in order to maintain the design aesthetics. At the same time, they managed to turn the suppliers of the materials and processes into co-sponsors of the product and significantly reduce costs while increasing product quality.

Compromise
With a conservative valuation of their own effort, design skills and the value of the product, the designers underestimated the price point. Even after receiving positive feedback on a higher price during the process, they ended up selling it at half that price. They went from testing the price of DKK600 to selling the lamps at DKK295 at the market.

Learning
The key take-away is to use your network and your network's network to get in touch with the people who can help you. Approaching suppliers as potential sponsors can open up different opportunities for trade and significantly improve your business case.

The designer's own key take-away
Palle pointed towards the value of reaching out, saying "If you need something, call and talk to someone." Anders reflected on the price, saying: "We should have gambled more on the price…been bold and said this one costs 800, because it is a kick-ass design." His key take-away was that fast decision making and going with one's gut feeling most of the time can get you far.
- Anne's take-away was the power of storytelling and the act of selling in a fair-like setup. "I've used my experience with building up an exhibition at a fair. Like how do you attract people? What story are you conveying?"

The business side of design: *Resources vs Business*

The objective is to sell the product. Therefore, the challenge is to engage with people as potential customers and not just users of a product. This challenges the embedded Scandinavian user-oriented approach to product development and design—especially the intrinsic designer-desire to solve problems for users and address real needs. You now have to balance the desire to do good with a business approach to making money. You must interact with potential customers to get feedback on proposals in order to improve the product and to understand whether they would be interested in buying it and what part of the product has the most value. In some way, it is a two-way interaction: trying to get feedback on the feasibility of a proposal while also promoting the idea of a purchase to the potential customer.

Case
Table Lamp 2

Designers: Sofus Amby Jørgensen & Mikkel Thomassen

This case is about using this challenge as an opportunity to learn quickly, learn about 'new' production technologies and integrate them with design quality to position the product in the market. In the bigger perspective, it is learning about the market's reaction to the product as a probe before taking it to the next level.

Define
The designers took a leap of faith into a product category suitable for an impulse purchase in a specific price range, and they focused on eliminating as many variables as possible as soon as possible. They also engaged in fast decision making.

From the very beginning, the designers were driven by the time pressure and the freedom of the challenge.

" *We were quite ready to race from the start; we knew we were under enormous time pressure and had very high ambitions. It was kind of a pressure test of design entrepreneurship, kind of a kick-off for us.*

The design team started to narrow down the variables and define the product based on gut feeling. The designers removed as many variables as possible, as fast as possible. Over lunch, the first day, they did ten drawings of different lamps. From that discussion and those drawings, they decided to do a table lamp. It is easier to make an impulse purchase on a small lamp that can be placed anywhere in a person's home.

" *Then, we started to look at different geometries—both in relation to what we think is cool design-wise, but also in order to not have too many elements to produce in the relatively short time frame. We choose a drawing we did on a napkin by the end of the first day, and we were in fact pretty close to a defined design."*

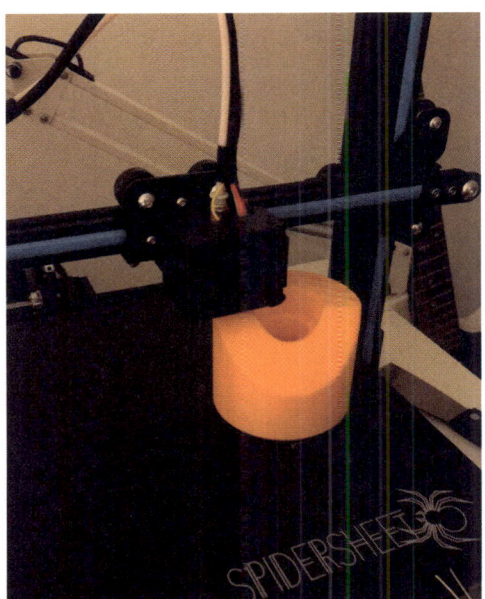

Design
With their ambition for a high design quality, the designers carefully positioned the design beyond DIY quality by embracing new techniques for manufacturing as an integrated part of the design.

The next step was CAD modelling and prototyping to prepare for the production.

> *We had some paper. If we need to make a lamp, then there are typical elements, like a base and a shade. We were considering how to simplify this to ease the production process. We started with a lot of paper and we had a light bulb, so pretty quickly we made a lampshade from the resources we had close by.*

The base of the lamp was the hardest element. It proved to be the most challenging for the design team. The designers were skilled at 3D modelling and printing. However, they strived for a higher design quality in terms of texture and materials than 3D plastic printing could produce. Moreover, they estimated that the production time of 20 3D prints would be too high.

> *We were pretty ambitious in the design. We wanted to work with materials we had never worked with before. We wanted to make something that you can't say "I am going to go and 3D print that or laser cut that or plot that myself". We wanted something that was difficult to replicate.*

Their dilemma was that they did not want to do something anyone could do in a wood workshop. However, they needed to be able to do it themselves.

> *We started to look into how we could design a base that we could 3D print, recast in silicone and cut so we would get a negative shape, where we could pour some kind of material in, like resin, porcelain or other stuff.*

They identified an employee from the workshop that was highly skilled and passionate about concrete casting techniques. They started to gather information about the timeframe for different types of concrete. Eventually, they got the needed assistance and acquired the basic knowledge to get started.

Make

A long and slow production phase that required fast decision making up front and continuously addressing unforeseen hiccups created opportunities for tweaking the value proposition and selling points.

Having learned about the concept of drying and hardening of concrete, the designers calculated the total time it would take to produce 20 units. They realised that the process barely fit within the deadline. They took a leap of faith early on and invested a large part of their budget in quick drying concrete and silicone materials for the mould. When they started the moulding process, the production created new problems. With no time to redo the mould, it forced them to reframe the problems into product features.

To begin with, we wanted uniform products. We wanted the concrete bases to look uniform and similar. However, we quickly realised we could not get the same finish or colour; there were many nuances that made variations. Then early on, we choose to embrace that they weren't 100% identical. So instead, we turned it into a feature. We started to experiment with different colours and finishes. And that also led to differences in the shade of the colours and the wood types.

The design team purchased paper in different colours and different types of wooden sticks. They stumbled upon their unique selling point of customising the product by accident, because of a variance in the production they could not disguise or ignore.

With a significant hardening time for the concrete and the fact that they only had one mould, the production time was the most significant activity. They did not have the time or money to make more moulds, so they had to spend more time setting up a continuous process of filling the mould, letting it dry for two hours, emptying it, then refilling it, etc. This was tedious and time-consuming. They also encountered assembly challenges they had not thought of until they put the lamps together, such as the lamp needed a chord under the base. The 20 lamps were ready to take to the market with only minutes to spare.

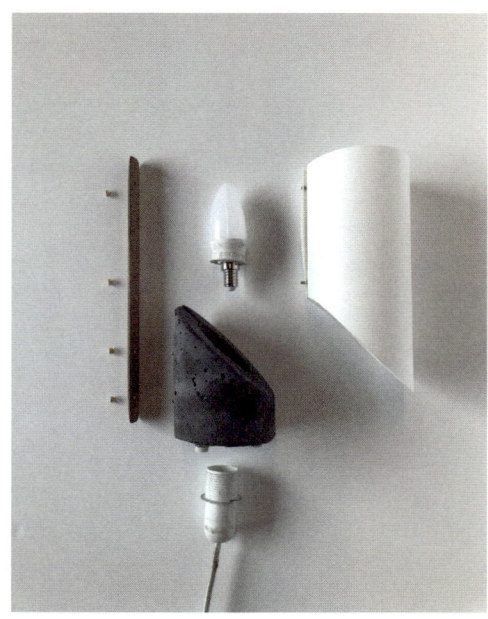

Sell

The team focused on creating a full customer experience around the sales situation, making a DIY trend easily accessible and leveraging customisation principles to cater to an impulse shopping situation by making it easy to match the product to the customer's home décor style.

While the concrete was hardening, the designers started to work on the customer experience aspect of the lamp. They embraced the product surface and colour variance that had been created by mistake in the production. They developed it into a concept around the DIY trend and the interest in vintage products. We all want to be unique in the 21st century, but we do not have the time to be as creative as we would like.

❝ So, we wanted to create another type of co-creation, the easy assessable way, where customers come to the booth, pick the parts and finishes they want and we build the lamp for them.... We built this table that you walked around. First you chose your concrete, then a piece of wood and then you walked further on and chose a shade. By the end, you had kind of created the lamp. And that created a kind of hype, and people started to queue up, because we were really slow at assembling the lamp.

The lamps were sold out in 45 minutes, and it was deemed a success. The lamps were priced at DKK 129. The designers aimed at breaking-even, not getting a large profit. In hindsight, the design team saw the Designers' Market success as a way to test if the product was sellable, hence functioning as a proof of business. They were also intrigued by the entrepreneurial approach to design but they were not satisfied with the product quality. With their experience in the production process, an improvement in the design and capital from the Designers' Market, they reinvested in round two. Six months later, they created a new batch, adding another product to the portfolio (a concrete wall clock) and they signed up for another market.

At another designers market they now charge a much more realistic price considering the workload required to produce the product and the product quality. It retails at DK 499.

Key Take Away

Let us look at what was significant in this table lamp case. What did the designers do successfully and what did they neglect, ignore or not prioritise?

Focus for this team was to leap into the production of 20 units while acquiring the skills of using a new manufacturing method. Defining the product category was almost a gut feeling allowing them to go into production planning mode from day two. This sent them on a trajectory of constantly oscillating between design details in the production with a 'locked' design and the business perspective and the value proposition needing to adapt to the developments. In the end, this merged into a coherent customer experience and effective promotional storytelling.

• • • • • • • • • • • • • • •

Succes
The designers managed to integrate clear design ambitions with a pivot in the value proposition and key selling point even when they were introduced to production failures and consistency issues. They turned these into a coherent value proposition and created the customer experience around the DIY selling points.

Compromise
The designers had to let go of their ambition to create uniform products and adopt a more pragmatic perspective: better to have a minimum-viable-product to sell than 20 "perfect" but incomplete products.

Learning
The key take-away is to trust your gut feeling and to not overcomplicate the definition of a customer; instead, it is important to focus on the purchasing situation. Framing as a learning experience in a bigger perspective is more rewarding.

The designer's own key take-away
Because the designers started a trajectory of entrepreneurship, this product was subsequently improved and successfully sold at the market. Mikkel's key take-away from the challenge was: "Execution, you need to act and try before you get results." Sofus added: "Embrace the responsibility of setting your own agenda."

Quality and consistency: *Production vs Market*

With a minimum of 20 units of a product, there is an expectation of consistency in quality when you bring products to market. The customer is not buying a unicum; they are purchasing a unit of a product. Even though many of the products in the cases presented here have some sort of hand-crafted value, there is still the expectation of consistency and uniform quality. In other words, the customer may choose any of the 20 units and expect the same product even if the colour or material varies.

With all the limitations in the setup, product quality and consistency are critical and can be hard to achieve. Are you able to manufacture 20 units of sufficient 'build-quality"?

Did they design for a business reality?

We wrote this book with the intention of pushing designers towards designing a product for a business reality using a pressure cooker framework.

Did they take business and the reality of business into consideration?
Did we succeed? The short answer is: Yes. But as usual, there are some nuances and more to be said. Because this setting forces the designer into a new role as a sole-owner, thus upsetting the "normal" imbalance between desirability, feasibility and viability, they have no experience with this new equilibrium. As seen in many of the cases, the design part of the process was not prioritised, and in some cases it did not exist at all. The enquiry and focus on the design were intended to enable the designers to identify something acceptable and sellable.

However, the business aspect became prominent in all the cases in the form of the business case. All the design teams focused on reaching a break-even point or getting some acceptable profit from the venture. Decision making about the details, features and materials were affected by the cost-benefit analysis of whether it would bring relevant value to the product within a budget. To that point, we were successful. The designers certainly understood that bringing a product to market requires continuous attention to the budget and the business case.

Did they solve real (larger) problems?
Not really. The products were all known products, mostly in the interior decor category, obviously related to the timeframe, but also the point of sale. Interior design products do not represent a key problem or need for a customer. But because they do not, they also represent a product category where most people are susceptible to inspiration and spontaneous purchases. Most of the products you can design and produce in ten days do not "solve larger problems" in a scale that designers are used to when given more time and fewer restraints.

Did they focus on what really matters?
Yes. None of the products are feature-loaded and over-complicated in terms of functionality. And in the process, the designers did not spend as much time interacting with users as they would have in a normal design process. The focus was on identifying the value proposition through sketches, models and 3D renderings. They did not explore additional needs or problems to address to expand the concept. They focused mainly on determining which variant or style of a product people responded positively to.

Did they care about how to make the product come to life?
Certainly! That was one of the most dominant activities in the process. It represented the biggest challenge for the designers. With the objective of making 20 units, all the cases show that this required a lot of consideration, time and significant resources. If they did not consider the construction, assembly and post-processing requirements when developing the concept, they certainly experienced the consequences of that in the production phase.

Photo: Quang Tran

Execution

this is my job now..

Advice for staging the challenge

If you are the host for staging such a challenge, we have a few words of advice. These are key points we believe are important for creating the prerequisites for the participants to embrace ownership of all the aspects and maintain the pressure in the pressure cooker.

Clarify the final event from the beginning
Make sure the participants know the conditions under which they can sell and promote their product. There are enough uncertainties as it is, and it is important that the participants know the format and possibilities at the point of sale so they can prepare their promotion material and determine how to display the product and develop a price strategy.

Don't set too many boundaries
The point is to allow for initiatives you could not think of yourself. Entrepreneurs do not need rules and regulations. The open playing field is part of creating the pressure cooker while simultaneously allowing for individual risk management. The participants will not over-commit and they can adjust their own level of ambition.

Timeboxing is key
The pressure cooker only works if there is a time limitation. That limitation includes the sales part, which should also have some sort of timeframe. Keep the challenge short and intense; allowing for more time than 2–3 weeks will just increase expectations and possibly introduce too much stress. Balance the time, so it seems almost impossible.

Advice for participating in the challenge

If you are planning to participate in this kind of challenge, we have summarised a few key words of advice. This is based on our combined experience to date and the reflections of the designers who have participated in the challenge.

Approach people as customers
Be systematic in your approach. For instance, try different price points with various groups of people, and try various price points within the same group of people. The point is you want to understand who will buy the product and what value it represents to them.

Call-to-action and pre-sell
Don't believe statements made without consequences. Think of ways to get small commitments or effort from the people you engage with to understand the real interest in the product. The best feedback is a commitment to purchase before production.

Design for manufacturing
Think forward. You are the one dealing with the design faults when fabricating the components and assembling the product. It may be worthwhile to consider how to manufacture and assemble all the components while in the design phase, doing so can prevent problems or time-consuming fixes later on.

Plan and prepare production
Think forward and think in terms of time-efficiency later in the process. "Luck favours the prepared", as they say. The more careful you prepare for production, the less time you will spend producing the products. Do not forget to account for post-processing activities, like sanding, polishing and perhaps colouring.

Market and promote from day 1
Combine your efforts to create attention and stand out from the crowd. When engaging with people, see them as potential customers and promote the event and yourself. Define how you will stand out from the competition, identify what will create attention and determine how your value proposition differs from your competitors.

Go all in
Do not hold back. Define your affordable loss, and push the envelope. This provides an opportunity to learn and test how much you can achieve under pressure. Playing it safe and not challenging yourself will probably not produce a desirable result.

Use your entire network
There is no limit to who you can involve. Successful entrepreneurs leverage their entire relevant network to contribute to some part of the venture. Do not think of a network as only the people you know directly; second degree people in your network might also be useful.

Focus on what matters the most
There is no need for extras that do not add value. Every time you engage potential customers or other stakeholders, try to identity what matters the most. What is the key selling point? What product feature or function (including aesthetics) would make the difference between polite feedback and an actual sale?

RESOURCE AVAILABILITY FOCUS

Resource WS

Personal knowledge and skills
As in effectuation, the starting point of the idea of making something should be rooted in the resources that are available. You are a large part of what is available. The first round of questions to answer includes:

<u>What can I do?:</u>

"What can I do" refers to your skills and competences. If you are particularly good with a CNC milling machine or casting objects in concrete, then that may be a starting point of generating ideas for a product.

Resource WS

What do I have knowledge of?:

"What do I have knowledge of?" This question triggers a search for insights and understanding of particular application areas. If you are part of a climbing club, then that might lead to clues for products and solutions relevant for that environment and target group.

What am I interested in?:

If you are interested in ceramics and interior design trends, then it may lead to the design and production of a set of bowls.

Resource WS

External network of opportunities
Searching your first- and second-degree networks might reveal access to information, materials or production capability, tools and processes. That search might reveal opportunities for adding resources to the pool. With limited financial resources available, you are encouraged to look for ways to add to your pool of resources through your network. So, in addition to the very few people that may have some materials available for the production of products, you should search your network for access to free or cheaper materials. There are also resources in the network, and that is where the last effectuation question comes in:

<u>Who do I know?:</u>

For example, the neighbour of someone's father might be a carpenter and she may be able to provide access to professional machinery for processing wood or maybe just be able to offer advice and help with the design and construction of objects made of wood. Looking through your network for opportunities to add resources to the project and can expand the potential solution space for "the product".

Resource WS

Financial resources

Obviously, you do not have unlimited funds, so it is important to apply the effectuation principle of "affordable loss".

What is affordable for you is a personal evaluation, and since the choice of product is free, you can calibrate this independently.

What is my affordable loss?:

PRODUCTION CAPABILITIES FOCUS

Production WS

Production of the product covers the entire process from sourcing materials, constructing the product, planning the production process, executing the steps in the production, maybe post-production processing, assembly and perhaps the logistics of transportation and packaging. Therefore, it is important to consider how to source of the materials and tools and how to determine the availability of help and perhaps the need for expertise. Please consider:

"Which materials do I have easy or cheaper access to?

Which materials need to be sourced? - And do I know any shortcuts?:

Which tools would be relevant?:

Production WS

Designing for production

The more time you spend in the design and concept development process thinking about the consequences for production, the easier it will be to actually produce 20 units. Make sure you detail your design and construction in the concept development phase, so you do not postpone the decision making until you are in the workshop production phase. Please consider:

Can you simplify the construction?:
(e.g., fewer components or fewer features)

Reducing complexity in the design will minimise the risk and time consumption in the production phase, and it will make it easier to plan and foresee the production process. Remember that every time you design one component, you will have to repeat the production process 20 times! For example, designing a lamp with 25 slats means you will have to produce 20 × 25 slats = 500 slats.

Production WS

Understanding the critical parts of your design may help you improve it and reduce the risk of failure in the production:

What is the most critical part in the current design? and How can I reduce the risk of something going wrong in the production?:

Designing things in 3D is not the same as putting things together physically in a sequence. Remember, laws of nature, like gravity, do not apply in 3D models, but they do apply in the real world. So please consider:

How do I assemble the components, and can I change the design to make it easier?:

Production WS

Planning

When you have to repeat every step 20 times, it will be wise to consider the sequence and order of these steps. Organising the production process can help save time and enable you to understand if you need to enlist help or assistance. It is a matter of aligning your resources with the activities and actions needed to meet the deadline. You might not know everything about every step or have the time or skill to perform all the required actions. So please consider:

Do I have the required skills/know-how? If not, how can I access it?:
(assistance, help with processes, tools)

What is the availability of tools, machines and perhaps timeslots in the workshop?:

Production WS

Thinking through the steps in the production may allow you to productively use idle time (like waiting for glue or paint to dry) to do other things, maybe attend to other steps in the production or marketing activities. Somethings can be done in parallel, while others require a sequence. So please consider:

How can I optimise time by organising the sequences?:

Usually, something will go wrong one way or another, or some steps will take longer than estimated. Getting an overview of the timeline and interdependencies between different steps is a good idea. It will also make it easier to adapt when you have you replan when you experience components breaking, glue that does not hold the product together, etc. So, please consider:

"What is the overall timeline?" and "What are the most critical deadlines for steps (gates) in the process?"

Production WS

Finally, consider the materials. You probably do not have an infinite amount of material and it also represents a cost, usually one that is significant. Optimising the use of materials is a combination of designing for production and planning the production. It may be that by changing the size of the product or a component 1 cm you may be able to fit 20 pieces into one sheet of MDF instead of 19. In that way, you may save the cost of an additional sheet by compromising slightly on the design. Or it may be that by carefully arranging the 20 cut-outs, you may be able to minimise waste and fit the cut-outs themselves into one sheet. So please consider:

How can I optimise the use of materials?:

You can think about either re-designing the product or carefully planning the use of materials.

Production WS

Fabrication and production
Working in the workshop and fabricating the components of a product may require some trial-and-error. You may not be able to foresee or have experience with all the processes and their outcomes. So, you may have some more unexpected work to do before reaching an acceptable result. Some things you can consider upfront or you may simply need to make a prototype to learn about the production processes and the quality of the outcome. So please consider:

Do the components need post-processing like surface treatment, sanding, painting, polishing, etc.?

What are the tolerances of the components in reality, and does this affect the assembly?:

Production WS

Budget
Before and during the production, you need a budget to maintain an overview of the project costs. This will also allow you to re-budget when problems occur due to unforeseen issues or if you decide to upgrade materials due to customer feedback. During the process, you should keep tabs on your expenses and inventory of your materials.

What is my budget for costs?:

You may also consider if it is possible to remove some of the items of your budget. Maybe you can acquire some of the materials for free, maybe they are leftovers from the production of other products.

BUSINESS CASE: MONEY FOCUSED

Business WS

Resonance: Understanding the real value
This is an important new perspective for you as an investor of resources and money into the product. This is not just about users and how they would use a product. It now becomes customer-centric and is about whether or not people would buy the product. So please determine:

What would make the customer buy the product, and what is the core value proposition?:

When you probe the ideas through sketches, 3D renderings, etc., there is a chance of a obtaining a systematic feedback loop that helps identify both the core value proposition and the corresponding target group. By probing the product idea in different communities, places and settings, there is a chance to learn about who responds positively to the product and who is indifferent to it. In addition to getting feedback on the product features, material and over all concept, there is a chance to learn more by understanding who responds. Thus, you can build an understanding of what characterises the target audience for the idea and which part of the proposal matters the most for potential customers.

Business WS

In this part of the process, you are also facing the question of variants if the feedback is not necessarily 100% conclusive. You might need to cater to different tastes. So, you may consider:

Is there a need to offer a variety of colours, materials and sizes?:

At the same time, the quest for feedback changes from approaching users to getting feedback on the product idea and features to understanding who will be interested in buying the product once it is available. With limited resources, this now becomes a quest for understanding which part, component or feature in the product is crucial for the customer.

Business WS

Budget
To keep track of the balance between investment, mostly expenses on materials, and the (potential) earnings, you need to make a budget. Be sure to include all materials and paid services.

With a budget of expenses, you can now adjust the unit price according to the feedback on price point, and vice versa. You need to adjust the budgeted expenses based on the price point feedback. Determining the break-even point, for example six units out of the 20, will also define the potential profit if the products is sold out.

Pricing is not only based on a mark-up of the cost of producing the product, it is also based on what potential customers are willing to pay for the value proposition embedded in the product. This latter point is the main, critical uncertainty in the process. That makes the pricing policy part of the risk assessment; how much do we dare ask for our products versus the desire to reach a break-even point and even make a profit? So please consider:

What should be the break-even point for the number of sold units?:

To improve the business case, expenses can be transformed from money to favours or other kinds of trade with stakeholders or suppliers. For instance, you can offer one unit of the product to a company that help with coating a component or bending and cutting steel plates.

CUSTOMER FOCUSED MARKETING + SALES

Market WS

Uncertainty of willingness

During the process, uncertainty is the main component in the risk you are willing to take. As suggested under the marketing price point, you can engage potential customers during the development process. This can be done systematically to develop the understanding of the target group by noting who responds positively. This includes who they are (profile), what part of the proposed product they respond most positively to (core value) and what they would be willing to pay for the final product (price point). This still leaves you with the uncertainty of whether the respondent was merely polite and not giving their honest opinion, or simply might not be attracted enough to the product to actually purchase it.

So, please consider:

What can I do to get potential customers to engage or show real interest?:

Call-to-action strategies, like pre-order or signing up for notifications, might help mitigate the uncertainty, but they cannot eliminate it.

Market WS

Marketing

Ideas and products can be great or even brilliant, but it does not matter if no one knows about them. You have to market and promote your products to the right audience to attract potential customers. This process does not have to wait until after the product is designed and produced. It can start before the concept is even settled by involving potential customers in testing the product ideas.

What additional actions can you take to call attention to your upcoming product?:

Market W5

Price point

In the same quest for understanding the core value proposition and the essence of the product concept, there is the question of price. What is the product worth to the target audience? There is a fluent relationship between this question and its answer depending on several parameters during the process.

A systematic approach to this can combine the understanding of who is being asked with trying different price points with the same type of people and different types of people. Thus, you can explore how much different target groups are willing to pay and where the critical price point is. When is it too expensive?

How can I systematically test the price point for my product?:

Sincerity is an important parameter. It is not that respondents are lying, but it requires no commitment to answer: "How much will you pay?" or "Will you pay DKK200 for this product?".

It may require some sort of call-to-action to test the potential customer's actual willingness to purchase the final product. It can be a simple offer to email the potential customer when the product is available or taking pre-orders.

Market WS

Profiling
The response depends on "who" is asked. Respondents will evaluate a proposal based on their own preferences and sometimes skills. For example, you may experience that if people are in the creative professions, they would not pay much for aesthetics or things they could make themselves. People from non-creative professions would pay a higher price for the same proposed product, because they could not make it themselves; thus, they value the form, expression and aesthetics of the product higher.

Is there a pattern in the responses that can help identify a customer profile of who is more interested in purchasing the product?:

This also depends on the means of communication. Showing potential users or customers a hand-sketch requires more imagination from the respondent. The respondent might either take the sketch at face value and not be willing to pay much for the product, or the respondent might imagine a final product with a professional level of fit and finish and therefore be willing to pay more—at least at the time of being questioned. However, that may change when they see the final result.

Market W3

Promotion

In addition to the embedded promotion through the involvement of potential customers, you are free to engage in other activities to promote your product and the market more broadly. This can include physical and local activities, such as making posters of the product and hanging them on campus. It can be combined with a model of the product, when available.

Additional promotional ideas also include using social media and other internet tools. All the students in the class may share an interest in getting people attracted to the market event. They could all be interested in supporting a joint Facebook campaign targeting certain groups in the local area. Instagram stories displaying product ideas or even versions of the product can be used to probe for feedback and generate attention.

Some of the designers mentioned in this document leveraged their network and used existing web shops to promote their products and maybe even obtain pre-sales or take reservations. So, please consider the following:

Which means can I use and what activities can I do to promote my product before the market to create awareness and interest?:

Market WS

Point of sale (channel)
The venue may be like any other fair or market; you will be allocated an area and a time slot. The venue and time slot provide some intrinsic audiences, the students in the building and the staff going for lunch. Attracting any other crowd requires additional effort from the students (see promotion).

There are no predefined tools, tables or other means of setting up a booth. You are free to create, build and setup your own point of sale at the venue. This sets a challenge of attracting customers to a booth, displaying the product and communicating the core value proposition and pricing.

What can I do to attract customers to my booth, and how do I showcase my product?:

Market W5

Sales pitch

Selling a product is not a passive activity. Products do not fly off the table into the hands of customers. You have to become a salesperson and leverage the visual material (like posters), the style and feel of the booth and the product itself to actively communicate the core value of the product and try to make it relevant for potential customers. This is not a trivial activity. It is challenging to make the story of the product come alive in the right version for the person standing in front of the booth. It is essential to rehearse the pitch and develop an understanding of what 'hooks' the different customers. With the limited time slot, the pressure is high. Inactivity may be punished by customers walking by, so students need to reach out without scaring people away.

What are the three main selling points of my product?:

Some people add videos to their communication, showing either functionality or perhaps a video from the production process of the product to try to communicate the "made by hand" value of the product. So, to sharpen your message, please consider:

What is the storytelling aspect of this product, and how do I stage it?:

Market WS

Packaging

Once you have a potential customer at your booth and you are engaged in the process of a sale, you do not want the customer to disengage because he/she cannot leave your booth with the product in hand.

Lamps, ceramics, glass, etc. all have a degree of fragility and, in general, there is a convenience issue when people are at a market: they do not want to carry the product in their hands. So, packaging the product may help eliminate that purchase barrier and, at the same time, represent a branding opportunity. So, please consider:

How does the customer get the product home?:

Packaging in general is a large part of the point of sale; it helps protect the product during transport and it offers space to promote and brand the producer and include instructions, feature selling points, etc.

References

Akin, Omer, and Chengtah Lin. 1995.
"Design Protocol Data and Novel Design Decisions."
Design Studies
16 (2): 211–236.

Brabham, D. C., 2021.
Moving the crowd at threadless.
Information, Communication & Society
13(8), pp.1122-1145.

Brown, T. and Katz, B., 2011.
Change by design.
Journal of Product Innovation Management
28(3), pp.381–383.

Buijs, J. (2012).
The Delft Innovation Method A Design Thinker's Guide to Innovation.
In DS 71: Proceedings of NordDesign 2012, the 9th NordDesign conference
Aalborg University, Denmark.
22-24.08. 2012.

Cross, Nigel. 2006.
Designerly Ways of Knowing.
London: Springer Verlag.

Dorst, Kees, and Nigel Cross. 2001.
"Creativity in the Design Process: Co-Evolution of Problem-Solution."
Design Studies
22 (5): 425–437.

Dreyfus, S. E., & Dreyfus, H. L. 1980.
A five-stage model of the mental activities involved in directed skill acquisition.
California Univ Berkeley Operations Research Center.

Knapp, J., Zeratsky, J., & Kowitz, B. 2016.
Sprint: How to solve big problems and test new ideas in just five days.
Simon and Schuster.

Krippendorff, Klaus. 2006.
The Semantic Turn—A New Foundation for
Design.
New York: CRC Press/Taylor and Francis Group.

Lawson, B. 2018.
The Design Student's Journey: Understanding how Designers Think.
Routledge.

Lawson, B. and Dorst, K., 2013.
Design expertise.
Routledge.

Laursen, L. N., & Haase, L. M. 2019.
The shortcomings of design thinking when compared to designerly thinking.
The Design Journal
22(6), 813-832.

Laursen, L. N., & Tollestrup, C. 2017.
Design thinking-a paradigm.
In DS 87-2 Proceedings of the 21st International Conference on Engineering Design (ICED 17) Vol 2:
Design Processes, Design Organisation and Management, Vancouver, Canada
21-25.08. 2017 (pp. 229-238).

Österwalder, A. and Pigneur, Y. 2010.
Business model generation: Handbook for visionaries, Game changers and challengers.
Hoboken, NJ: John Wiley & Sons.

Ries, E. 2011.
The lean startup.
New York: Crown Business, 27.

Rittel, Horst W. J., and Melvin M. Webber. 1973.
"Dilemmas in a General Theory of Planning."
Policy Sciences 4 (2): 155–169.
doi: 10.1007/BF01405730.

Sarasvathy S. D. 2008.
Effectuation- Elements of entrepreneurial expertise.
New York: Edvard Elgar Publishing

Schön, D.A., 1983.
The reflective practitioner.
New York, 1083.

Suchman, L. A. 1987.
Plans and situated actions: The problem of human-machine communication.
Cambridge university press.

Ulrich, K. T. 2003.
Product design and development.
Tata McGraw-Hill Education.

Photo: Sebastian Hougaard Andersen